IT'S JUST CANCER,

GOD IS STILL GOD!

IT'S JUST CANCER,

GOD IS STILL GOD!

PASTOR RONALD A. PALMER

ARPress
ILLUMINATING IDEAS.
EMPOWERING VOICES

ARPress
45 Dan Road Suite 5
Canton MA 02021

Hotline: 1(888) 821-0229
Fax: 1(508) 545-7580

Ordering Information:

Quantity sales. Special discounts are available on quantity purchases by corporations, associations, and others. For details, contact the publisher at the address above.

Printed in the United States of America.

ISBN-13:   Paperback   979-8-89330-159-5
              eBook   979-8-89330-160-1

Library of Congress Control Number: 2024901848

TABLE OF CONTENTS

THE INTRODUCTION TO CANCER:

My family has long been acquainted with cancer! I was nine years old, and we were living in Winner, South Dakota in 1951 when I was "introduced" to it. I remember it very clearly. My Mother had just got the mail and she was walking up the front steps when she stopped on the small porch to open and read a letter she had just received. Suddenly, she began to cry.

I was playing in the front yard, and the suddenness of her crying, and the intensity of it, got my attention in a big way. I asked her what was wrong, and she said, "Oh, Ron. I just received a letter from my sister, and she said my mother has cancer." When I asked her what that was, she controlled her crying and told me it was a "a disease that people died from." That was my "introduction" to cancer.

I guess Grandma passed away about two or three years later. Her condition kept getting worse, and she finally succumbed to it. We went to see her a few times before she passed away. Each time I saw her I still didn't quite understand. She lay there in bed, very calm, and talked to the family. There was no "visible" evidence that she was dying, and that's what was puzzling to me.

Each time we went to see her, she was very noticeably weaker but that really didn't register much on me because there was no visible evidence such as bleeding, vomiting, or any such thing. Then she was gone, and being a young kid, there wasn't a lot of dwelling on it, and soon it was just something of the past. I was preoccupied in important "kid stuff" like school, playing, and such like: so, it faded from memory rather quickly. The only thing I realized was that we didn't go to Grandma's anymore. That, too, soon passed from any prominent memory.

The next exposure to cancer, dubbed the "silent killer," was with my Dad's brother, Uncle Gene. Our family was never close to Uncle Gene and his family. We used to go visit them once in a while, because he was

Dad's brother. None of the kids liked any of their family, however, so it was more of an "endurance contest" than a visit for us.

We received a letter from them telling us that Gene had throat cancer. It really didn't surprise us because Dad said Gene would drink his coffee right when it was poured into his cup scalding hot. Dad said he didn't know how Gene could do that, but that he had done it for years. They sent us a brief letter telling us that he had died of cancer.

I worked in surgery as a surgical technician for forty-eight years. Forty-one of those I was bivocational, pastoring small Churches while working in surgery as a secular job. During that time, I worked on hundreds of cancer surgeries. Some of them were really gruesome cases. I especially detested the cases where someone had waited too long to see the doctor because they were "afraid the doctor would tell them it was cancer." By the time they came in it was too late to save them.

I didn't detest the surgery itself, because I always actually loved surgery as a vocation. Even when some people were beyond healing, and some even died on the operating table, I really liked the surgery because we were doing all we could do to help people. I thanked God, and I still do, for the skills and abilities He had given me to help people. What I detested about those cases was the foolishness of the people who waited too long to come in for help and ended up dying because of it.

If you, or one of yours, has a problem that could be cancer, please go and see about it, regardless of how afraid you may be about the report. A month, or just a few months, could make the difference that could extend that life for years.

PASTORING AND CANCER:

I began Pastoring a small Church in Bellflower, California in May of 1971. There was an elderly woman in our congregation by the name of Sister Burnett. She was a sweet Christian lady who was exceptionally faithful in coming to Church. She never missed a Sunday for over fifteen years in a row and had the Sunday School attendance pins to show it.

Towards the end of my first year there she passed away from recurrent breast cancer. I held her service, and at the service I met her brother Wirt. He was a very likable old fellow of about 83 or 84 years old. We became very good friends after that service and were so for about three years or so before Wirt had to go to an assisted living home.

Wirt was not a Christian, and although he was very cordial and friendly, he made it very clear that he was not interested in any of "that stuff." Perhaps that's why we got along so well. I never tried to preach to Wirt. I just lived, and talked, my faith when we were together, and he never objected to anything I said.

Wirt had some terrible experiences when he was a young man. He married a lady he loved very much, and they had one baby. That was his son. One day, when the baby was just an infant, Wirt's wife walked in and told him she was through. She didn't want to be married anymore, didn't want him anymore, and didn't want the baby anymore.

She walked out on them and got a divorce. She never came back. Wirt took his baby to his sister, who was not married, and asked her if she would raise the baby as her own. He promised to provide everything for them, and that's the way the family "grew up." Pauline (Wirt's sister) never married, nor did Wirt ever marry again.

I met his son at Pauline's service, and we struck up a friendship right away. He was in his mid-fifties or so and would come out and visit Wirt every year. Whenever he came, he would stop and visit me, and we would talk about Wirt's need to be saved, among other things.

He moved Wirt to a rest home in Minneapolis where they could be near each other, and after a few years he stopped by on a visit and told me Wirt had passed away. He said, "By the way Pastor, Dad accepted Jesus before he went, and the last time I talked to him he said he wanted you to know." Now, when I look back on it, I don't see Pauline's cancer as something to be afraid of, or to be remorseful over, but as a catalyst that brought her family and me together. That resulted in several years of dear and precious friendship; and eventually to Wirt being saved.

The next experience I had with cancer was a few years later. It was our fourth year of ministry at the Downey Avenue Free Will Baptist Church. We had an older lady coming to our Church faithfully, but her husband wouldn't come for any reason. Her name was Mozelle, and his was Reggie. I guess they must have been in their seventies, but they seemed quite old to my "extensive" thirty-three years.

I was talking to Mozelle one day and I asked her why Reggie never came. She just shrugged her shoulders and said he just wasn't interested. I told her I wanted to come by and meet him some evening. She said, "Preacher, you do what you feel like doing, but let me warn you. He ran the last three preachers from this Church off and told them to never come back." I just told her I would wait for the Lord's leadership, then stop by some evening. She just shrugged, and said, "Well, I warned you."

A few weeks later, my wife and I were on a visitation one Thursday evening. We called on three families and none of them were home. She said, "Well, we might as well go home." All of a sudden, the Lord prompted me, and I said, "Let's go visit Reggie and Mozelle."

She said, "You remember what Mozelle told you about Reggie and the last three Preachers, don't you?" I said, "Yes, but I just feel led of the Lord to go visit them right now." Arlee, (my wife) just smiled and said, "Okay," so off we went.

They lived in a trailer park about four blocks from the Church. We drove over and went up to the door and I knocked. Mozelle opened the door and stood there looking rather shocked. Reggie said, "Who is it, Mozelle?" She said, "It's my Preacher and his wife." Reggie said, "Well, invite them in."

We stepped into the room and said "hello" to Reggie. He pointed to a chair beside him and said, "Have a seat, Preacher." I told him thank you and sat down as Mozelle and Arlee took seats in the kitchen about ten feet from us. Reggie reached down beside his chair and brought up a tall can of beer. He looked at it rather self-consciously, and said, "Well Preacher, I'd offer you one, but I don't suppose you'd accept."

I said, "No thanks, but you go ahead and enjoy yours while it's cold. When I was drinking, I never enjoyed them when they got warm." He looked at me and said, "You don't mind?" I said, "No, Reggie, I don't mind at all. This is your home, and you do what you want. I didn't come here to question your drinking; I came here to visit you and get acquainted."

He said, "Well, you go right ahead Preacher." A few minutes later he lifted his beer again, hesitated, then took a small sip. He lifted it again a bit later, hesitated, then set it back down without drinking any. We visited for about forty-five minutes, then I told them we needed to go. We got up and went to the door with Mozelle and Reggie said, "Preacher, you are welcome to come back anytime, and talk to me about anything you want to." I just told him, "Thanks, Reggie," and we left.

A few weeks later, Mozelle told me Reggie was in the hospital with cancer. I went up to visit him and found him alone in his room. I just began to get into a personal conversation with him when the door opened, and Mozelle and some family walked in. As soon as she saw me, she stopped, and with a real pained expression said, "I'm sorry, I didn't mean to interrupt." Reggie spoke up and said, "You're not interrupting anything. We were just talking. Come on in." I told Reggie I would go and come back another time.

The next night we had an extension class from our college that was being taught at our Church on Tuesday nights. I really felt the Lord impressing me to go see Reggie right away. At the break, I told the teacher what the situation was, and said I had to leave the class and go immediately. He told me to go and said the class would pray for me.

I left and went to the hospital. There was a table in front of the elevator and a nurse was sitting behind it. I told her I needed to see Reggie, and she told me she was sorry, but visiting hours had ended twenty-five minutes before. I dropped my Bible on the table in front of her and said, "Lady, I am a Pastor and there is a man upstairs dying with cancer. I don't need visiting hours! I am going up and see him right now." She sat back, and with her eyes big in surprise said, "Yes sir, he's in room……" and I said, "I know the room."

I went up and slipped into his room. I called his name softly and he answered. I told him I was there to visit with him. He responded, "Preacher, I don't want to visit with anyone right now. I am in a lot of pain, and all I want is to be left alone so I can go to sleep. You leave and come back some other time."

I said, "Okay, Reggie, I'll go. Mozelle said the doctors told you what your condition is now." He told me they did, and he knew he just had a few days left to live. I said, "Reggie, I just came by to tell you that you are getting ready to take the longest journey any person ever takes, and that is the journey into eternity. I wanted to tell you about a friend of mine named Jesus Who would really like to take that journey with you, so you don't have to go alone."

He said, "Yeah, Yeah, well you leave and come back and tell me some other time." I simply told him "Okay" and I left. I went home because the class was over at the Church. I told my wife what had happened and we prayed for Reggie.

The next morning, after a very fitful night, I got up and went to work. All day Reggie was really on my mind. I got home about four in the afternoon and the phone rang just after I walked into the house. It was one of the ladies from my Church, and she said, "Pastor did you hear the news about Reggie Hambrick?" I told her I had not because I had just gotten home from work and was going up to see him right away.

She said, "Reggie died this morning about nine thirty." My heart just sank, and then she said, "But, did you hear what happened just before he died?" I tried to have patience, feeling as I did, and told her

I hadn't heard anything since I had just gotten home. That's when she told me "The rest of the story."

She said, "Mozelle called me and said about nine o'clock Reggie told her to run, not walk, out and get the Chaplain. He told her to get the Protestant Chaplain, and not the Catholic one. She said she took off down the hall running as fast as she could to the Nurse's station and told them to call the Protestant Chaplain for Reggie."

Then Mozelle told her "A few minutes later the Protestant Chaplain rushed into the room and asked Reggie if he could help him. Reggie told him that "his Pastor" had come in to see him the night before to tell him about his friend Jesus Who wanted to go with him through eternity, but that he was in too much pain to listen at that time. He asked the Chaplain if he could tell him about his Pastor's friend Jesus. The Chaplain said yes, and minutes later they prayed, and Reggie accepted Jesus. Fifteen minutes later, Reggie died."

The lady who was telling me this over the phone said, "Well, what do you think of that Pastor?" I told her it was great news. My heart felt like it was going to burst with gratitude for God being so specific and personal. I had a quick prayer and said, "Thank you so much, Lord. That is as close as I ever want it to be." I told Arlee the news and we rejoiced in the graciousness of the God we serve.

Looking at that sequence of events showed me that cancer has the ability to attack the Christian and devastate the body, *but in reality, cancer cannot defeat the Christian, nor take their life. The Bible teaches us that God gives life, and He is the only one who can take life.* He uses cancer just as he uses heart attacks, diabetes, car wrecks, or any other way by which people die. They are all just "vehicles" He uses to usher us into eternity. When we have prepared ourselves for eternity by accepting Jesus Christ as our Savior and Lord, we are never defeated by cancer, nor anything else in life.

Thee Bible tells us in Romans 8:37, "Nay, but in all these things we are more than conquerors through Him that loved us." That, my friend, is not defeat in any way, shape, form, or fashion. That is victory in the highest form possible. In a moment Reggie went from being in a hospital bed ravaged with cancer to being in Heaven exalted in glory with Jesus.

After all, "........*it is JUST cancer ... ...,*" *but Jesus is salvation, and deliverance, and healing, and blessing.....* and the list goes on and on and on! Whether it is a Corrie Ten Boom who was saved at her mother's knee at five years old, and went through the horrors of the Holocaust, or a Reggie Hambrick who went into glory just fifteen minutes after he was saved; what really matters is personally knowing Jesus as Savior and Lord. That's where victory comes to us. As Paul said in I Corinthians 15:57, "But thanks be to God, which giveth us the victory through our Lord Jesus Christ." He gave it to us (past tense), it belongs to us (present tense), and it will always remain with us (future tense) if we will continue on with faith in Christ.

CANCER IN THE FAMILY

The next experience I remember having with cancer hit a lot closer to home. I had married Arlee, and my younger brother Russ had married Arlee's younger sister Bonnie, back in 1964. In 1975 we found out that their mother, Erma, had cancer, and we heard that she was in very bad shape and was expected to die within a few days. We lived in Los Angeles County in California, and Erma lived in Livingston, Montana. Russ and I talked it over and decided I would take Arlee and Bonnie and go to Livingston, while he stayed and worked to help pay for the trip. It being in February, he figured he got the best end of the deal.

We got to Bozeman where Erma was in the hospital and found she was not expected to live through the night. She had cancer of the bowel and when they gave her radiation treatment for it, they over did the treatment and burned the bowel. They were not aware of that until she got sick from the bowel and was on death's door. That's when they notified the family. It was evident she was dying from the bowel complications, and not from the cancer, but it was a result of the cancer.

When we got to the hospital, it was in the evening. We went to Erma's room, and she was so weak she could not pull the sheet up over herself. The girls did that, and we sat down and visited her. She almost had to gasp for breath, and she said the doctor told her she wasn't expected to live through the night.

I said, "Erma, you know what your condition is. I know you have never been personally interested in Christianity, but in a very short time you are going to be facing the Lord. Could I tell you about Jesus Who can change your life and assure you that you are ready to go?" She said, "yes," and I explained from the Bible how to be saved.

When I had finished explaining it to her, I asked if she would like to pray with us and receive Jesus as Savior. Again, she said yes, and we joined hands and prayed; and Erma was a new "babe in Christ." She was relaxed and smiled as she told us "Thank you."

It was nearing the end of visiting hours and suddenly the Lord impressed me to say something that would sound totally unrealistic. I said, "Erma, I want to pray for you, and ask the Lord to heal you and extend your life." She looked at me and after hesitating for a while, she said, "Alright, if you want to."

Arlee, Bonnie, and I joined hands, and I prayed a simple prayer for the Lord to raise Erma up, restore her health, and extend her life. There was nothing dramatic, novel, nor pretentious, just a simple prayer of faith. We went back to where we were staying and had a good night's rest.

The following morning, we came back at about 9:00 to tell her we had to leave to get back to California for my job and the Church. We got back to Erma's room, and it was empty, with the bed all made up. That was rather startling to us because of what the doctor had said about her not living through the night.

The girls asked if that meant she had died. I told them I didn't know, but we could ask someone. We stepped into the hallway, and I looked around for a nurse. What we saw startled all three of us.

Up the hall Erma and a nurse were walking down toward her room. Erma was walking along pushing her I.V. pole with one hand and holding her gown closed with the other. The nurse was walking behind her, watching so she wouldn't have any problems.

We waited until Erma got settled in bed, then went in to visit her. We asked how she was doing, and she said she was fine. She said the doctor had come in that morning and was astonished at how much she had improved through the night. He examined her and asked what had happened. She told him that her son-in-law, who was a preacher, had prayed for her, with her two daughters last night.

The doctor did not understand how it was possible, but said she had gotten so much better, so fast, that he was going to discharge her to go home the next afternoon. We learned later, (we left that afternoon) that she was released and went home the next day, to the surprise of the whole medical staff. She lived until December of 1989, which was just short of fifteen years, when she died of a different type of cancer. But that is another part of the story.

In July of 1978 I had another encounter with cancer. I flew to Kansas City to our annual conference. As I walked into the conference center, and started across the floor, I heard someone call my name real loud. I turned and saw a friend of mine who pastored a large Church of ours in Bakersfield, California.

He waved me over to where he was talking to another fellow. His name was Claudie Hames, and I said, "Hello, Claudie, how are you doing?" He said, "Hello, Ron," then turning to the fellow he had been talking to, he said, "This is the guy I was telling you about Dan. If anyone will go talk to your sister-in-law Ron is the one."

Rather baffled, I said, "What are we talking about?" Claudie said, Ron, this is Dan Dodson, and I'll let him tell you." Dan proceeded to tell me that he had a twin brother somewhere in my area of Los Angeles. He said his brother's name was Don, and Don's wife Audrey was in a hospital somewhere in my area dying of cancer. He said the doctors said she was not expected to live through that weekend, and he (Dan) wanted someone to talk to her about Jesus before she died. Neither Don, nor Audrey, nor their two teenagers were Christians.

I told him I'd be glad to go and visit her when I flew home that Thursday. I asked him which hospital she was in, and he said he didn't know, but it was in the North Long Beach area somewhere. We had an excellent conference, which was scheduled to end Thursday at noon. I had my flight home scheduled for the afternoon of Thursday and was planning on going then. Wednesday night was our biggest service, being the Mission service, and all through the service God kept dealing with me about Audrey Dodson.

As soon as service was ended, I called the airport and explained what the situation was. I asked if I could get my Thursday afternoon flight changed to that Wednesday night, and God blessed, and they were happy to do it.

I asked two of my friends from California if they could get me to the airport and they said yes. Fortunately, there were no highway Patrol cars on the freeway as we went. I grabbed my suitcase, told my friends goodbye, and rushed across the airport terminal just in time to hear the lady at the desk say, "Last call for flight to Long Beach, California." I yelled and told them to hold that flight and rushed up the loading ramp. The stewardess said, "Good Evening, Sir. You cut that one very close. Two more minutes and we would have had the doors closed."

I found my seat, sat down, and had a very sincere, silent prayer thanking the Lord for His grace and provision. A few hours later we touched down in Long Beach, and an hour later I was home; with Audrey Dodson still heavy on my heart.

The next morning, I got up and as soon as I was ready for the day, I got the phone book and turned to "hospitals." I decided to begin with the hospital nearest the Church and work outward from there. The first one I came to was The Doctor's Hospital of Lakewood, about two miles away. I asked if they had a patient by name of Audrey Dodson, and the operator said, "Yes, we do. Would you like me to dial her room for you?" I said, "No thank you, ma'am, I'm on my way up to see her right now."

Within a half hour I was there, and it turned out to be the same hospital I had gone to see Reggie in before. I found Audrey in her room alone, and I introduced myself to her, telling her about my meeting with her brother-in-law Dan a few days before.

Just as we began talking, the door opened and her husband and two children walked in, just like it happened with Reggie. Audrey introduced me to Don and their kids, and it was like I was looking at Dan. I knew they were twins but didn't know they were identical twins, or the closest thing to them that I ever saw. I told them I would go and let them visit and I could return and visit with Audrey the next day, which I did.

The following day I returned and again found Audrey alone. This time there were no interruptions during our discussion. I asked her if the Doctors had said anything about her condition. She began crying, and said, "Yes, they said they didn't expect me to live through this weekend." I asked her if I could tell her how much God loved her, and through the tears she smiled and said, "Please do!"

I told her about my trip to the conference in Kansas City, and how Claudie had also gone. I told her about him introducing me to Dan, and my conversation with Dan. I told her about my early trip home so I could be sure to find her and talk to her. I told her, "You see, Audrey, God loves you so very much that He took a minister from Bakersfield, and one from Bellflower, and sent them both to Kansas City. There the one from Bakersfield, who knew Dan, introduced him to me; and then God brought me back to talk to you about Jesus."

She again began to cry, and said, "I had no idea He loved me so much." I talked to her about Jesus and being saved; and asked her if she would like to pray right then and be saved. Five minutes late she was a brand-new Child of God. I then prayed for the Lord to bless her during this trying time she was going through.

Audrey surprised the doctors by living through the weekend, and her condition improved so much that they dismissed her to go home under hospice care. To the amazement of the doctors, and the family, she lived until just after Christmas. She lived from the third week of July to the last week of December, which was five months with her family longer than the doctors imagined possible. I stand in awe and amazement at how great and gracious God is.

Let me go back in the story a bit and finish elaborating on the miraculous working of God, which is the most exciting part of it. The Sunday after Audrey was saved in the hospital, we heard nothing from the family. The following Sunday Don and their sixteen-year-old son, and thirteen-year-old daughter walked in and sat down on the second pew from the front.

The following Sunday they came in again and sat in the same place, really paying attention during the service. On the third Sunday they came again, and when I gave the invitation after service, Don stepped out and came to the altar. Right behind him came his daughter, and behind her came his son. They all said they wanted to be saved, and fifteen minutes later, they were!

Once again, the destructiveness of cancer lost out to the grace of God as four people (an entire family) got saved just because cancer had attacked one of them. A physical life was ended because of cancer, but four Spiritual lives were given to four sinners who repented and shall spend eternity in glory because of it. *That is Victory, proving "….it is JUST cancer…." And God is STILL God!!*

About the time I was ministering to Audrey Dodson, one of the ladies of our Church told me about another woman who was dying of cancer. She was a young Mexican woman of about twenty-two who had a little boy that was about three years old, and she was in the beginning of her ninth month of pregnancy with their second baby.

I went up to see her and to minister to her. Her name was Crystal, and she said she was a Catholic and had prayed a lot, but she was still very afraid. She told me it wasn't just afraid of dying, which she said was very true, but also for the baby she was expecting. She told me the doctors had come in and told her she needed to allow them to abort the baby so they could give her chemotherapy and radiation without them disfiguring the baby.

Speaking through her tears, she asked me what she should do. I calmed her down and said I wanted to talk to her about Jesus, and what He could do. She agreed and I explained to her about how she could get saved and let Jesus take the fear of dying away. She was very responsive, and a few minutes later she prayed and was wonderfully saved. She looked at me, smiling through the tears, and said, "I'm no longer afraid of dying. I'm not afraid at all, Pastor, I am just so happy."

She began crying again and said, "But what can I do about my baby? I don't believe in abortion, and in fact, I have been raised to believe it is evil. So, what can I do?" I asked her if she truly meant what she prayed when she received Jesus. She very strongly affirmed that she believeth it with all her heart. I then said, "Crystal, why don't we pray and trust the baby's welfare to Jesus? You can refuse the abortion and let Jesus protect your baby from all the radiation, chemotherapy, and all of the other medical treatments you will receive."

She agreed and we prayed again. I simply asked God to bless Crystal with a safe and healthy pregnancy, and an easy delivery of a perfectly healthy baby. I was up to see her several times in the next month, and each time she was in good spirits, healthy, and happy. She said she was taking the treatments but had refused to have an abortion. The doctors didn't like it any but had to abide with her decision.

When her time came, she delivered a beautiful little baby girl, who was perfect in every aspect. She said she had no problems during the last month, nor during the delivery. Of course, the doctors were amazed, and they told her so. She responded by telling them she was not at all amazed. She told them she had accepted Jesus and was saved, then her Pastor had prayed for her and the baby that Jesus would take care of them; and He did. So, she didn't find that was amazing.

I visited with her a couple days after she delivered and saw the baby. It was absolutely beautiful and could have done real justice to the Gerber Baby Food commercials. While I was visiting her, she started crying again. Puzzled, I asked her what the problem was. She said, "Pastor the doctors said I only have about one to two months left to live. I am going to be discharged home tomorrow, and I want to come to your Church and hear you preach at least once, but I can't."

I asked her why she couldn't, and she told me it was because she had gained so much weight during the last month of her pregnancy; and taking the radiation and chemotherapy. She said she had gained forty-five pounds and couldn't get into any dresses.

I told her she didn't need to wear a dress because the Lord was interested in the condition of her heart, and not in what she was wearing. She smiled through her tears again, and said, "I know that's true. I realize it in my heart, but I was raised to wear a dress to Church as a Catholic, and since I've been saved, I want to honor Him more than I ever did before. That's why I need to be able to wear a dress."

She looked at me very seriously and said, "Pastor, would you pray that God will help me lose this weight so I can get into one of my dresses and attend Church at least once before I die?" It was my turn to be amazed and I sat there looking at this beautiful young woman in her early twenties, dying of cancer as she sat there holding her perfect baby girl; having been saved just over a month. Yet, having the faith in Jesus to believe God would answer her prayer for weight loss.

What did I do? I took her hand, and prayed a simple, sincere prayer of faith for her to lose weight and be able to come to Church in a dress before she went to Heaven. The reason I prayed a simple, sincere prayer (which I always try to do) was because that was a moment in time that was too holy and sacred to do anything else. I could only see her, the baby, and myself in that room; but I could feel the presence of others.

I left her and the baby in the hospital and went home. I heard that she had been discharged the day following and went home, presumably under home care. The Sunday after she was discharged, she was too weak to get out of bed from what I heard. The second Sunday evening after she was discharged, we were getting ready to start Sunday evening service.

The door opened and Crystal came in, being pushed in a wheelchair by her husband. She was holding her newborn daughter, and the little boy was walking beside daddy. I went back and met them, and she introduced me to her husband and son. I shook hands with the husband and welcomed them to service. Then I knelt down beside Crystal and looked at that beautiful baby girl, who could have so easily been aborted. I told Crystal I was so glad to see her. She handed the baby to her husband, smoothed her dress across her lap, and said, "Look, Pastor, I'm wearing one of my dresses that I wore before I went to the hospital. It fits me perfectly. I lost every bit of that weight I had gained, and I did it all in less than two weeks. Thank you for praying for me."

I, too, was so thankful for the divine privilege that was given to me, allowing me to pray for her. And, to realize once more, as I did many times before that, and many times after that, how specifically God answers prayer.

I heard she was unable to get out of bed the following weekend. The weekend after that she was having Church services in Heaven, in the presence of her Savior and Lord, Jesus Christ, the King of Kings and Lord of Lords.

I don't know what ever became of her husband and children, because I never saw them again. I do pray that I will one day be able to see them all there because of the awesome privilege I had of making another hospital call, on another cancer patient, who became another child of God through the process and why not? After all... it's *JUST cancer... ... and God is STILL God!*

In about May of 1988, I received a call from my oldest sister, Ruby, who lived in Lincoln, Nebraska. She told me she had been diagnosed with cancer of the liver. She said the doctor told her it was a single tumor about the size of a walnut, and the surgery should be as simple and effective as it could be for such a case. She didn't want it to be anything to make a big "to do" about, and there was no reason for us to come down there because it would be over before we got there. She said she would call right away and let us know the results.

Because of my twenty-four years (at that time) of medical experience, with twenty-three of them in surgery, I was in agreement with what she, and her doctors, had said. Then she gave me the good news. She said that her husband Grover, who was a self-proclaimed atheist/agnostic, and was openly antagonistic and hostile to anything my sister Ruby said about God, faith, Church, Bible, or anything else "religious" had changed his mind.

She said he told her, "If God will bring you through this surgery and back home, I'll go to Church with you and get my life straightened out." Well, the surgery went exceptionally well, and she was out of the hospital about the middle of June. She went through recuperation during the latter part of June and early July. She had recovered enough that she got up one Sunday morning and started getting ready for Church.

Grover came in and asked her what she was getting all "gussied up" for. She told him she was going to Church and reminded him of the promise he had made to start going with her if God brought her through the surgery and restored her health. He responded by telling her, "Don't give me all that "God junk." God had nothing to do with it. The doctors are the ones that healed you."

She asked him if he was going to get ready and go with her. He said he was not going to go with her then, or any other time, because he didn't believe in "that junk." He never did go to Church with her after that, which didn't turn out to be very long.

Arlee and I went to Kansas City for a conference in the third week of July. We stopped in to see Ruby on our way home and spent two days and nights with her. She told us all about her surgery and Grover's response, and said she just wished she could get out of the mess that her marriage had been for years, but she didn't believe in divorce.

I asked her how she was doing physically, and she rubbed her lower abdomen on the right side, and said, "Well, I've recovered and am feeling really good except for the pain here where they took the tumor out of my liver." I said, "Ruby, that's not where your liver is. Your liver is up under your ribs on the right side, not down in your abdomen." She asked me what would be causing her pain down there, especially after the doctors told her she would be feeling better than she had for the past ten years.

I told her I didn't know but she needed to go to the doctor when we left and tell him she wanted something done for the pain. She informed me she had been in to see him four times and each time he told her there was no problem. The last time he told her it may be psychosomatic.

I emphasized she needed to go in and insist on something to help, whether it was psychosomatic or not. I then told her to let him know she had talked to me, and I suggested a possible M.R.I. which is a type of x-ray but is much more intense and revealing on soft tissue than a regular x-ray or "cat scan."

A few days after we got home from our trip. I received a phone call from Ruby. She said she had gone to see her doctor again and told him what I said. He acknowledged it was a good idea, but that he would have to send her to Omaha to the university hospital for the MRI. She told me she would keep me informed as to what happened.

Just a few days later, I received another call from her. She said, "I'm afraid I have some bad news little brother. They did the MRI and it showed I have "small cell cancer" seeded throughout my intestines and my lungs." I asked how long they had given her, and she said, "They said I had from two months to a year at the most."

I told her I thought they were wrong in their estimate. She asked me how long I thought it was and I told her from what she described. It sounded like it was in a later "stage" of the disease. She said they told her it was "Stage four" which is the worst stage there is. I said, "I'm sorry to hear that Sis, but from all the experience I have had with cancer in surgery, I would say you probably have from two weeks to two months left. You need to get your affairs in order, and let your family and friends know."

She thanked me for my truthfulness and my openness; and told me she already had her affairs settled as far as her will was concerned. She had done that when she was diagnosed with the Liver cancer.

That was in the first week of August of 1988, and on the twenty-ninth of August she called me again. She told me she was in the hospital dying, and the doctors didn't expect her to live over twenty-four hours. I told her there was no way we could make it back there in that time, and she asked me how long we would need.

I told her we would need at least three days in order to get our paychecks and make the arrangements with our jobs, besides the twenty-four hours needed to drive straight through with both of us driving. She simply said, "I'll wait for you, and see you when you get here."

On September 1 of 1988, three days after our phone call, Russ and I walked into the hospital in Lincoln at about 9:30 in the morning. I walked up to the Nurse and told her who we were there to see. She said, "Well, I'll take you back to see her, but she won't recognize you." I told her Ruby would definitely recognize us. Her reply was, "Well, her pain was so bad last night we had to increase her morphine four times. She is in a morphine induced coma and can't recognize anybody now."

I told her to take us to see her because she certainly will recognize us because she is waiting for us. She looked at me like she thought I was "several bricks short of a full load," and took us back to Ruby. Before the nurse left, I stepped up and took Ruby's hand. She was sound asleep and was groaning because of the pain.

I took her hand and spoke her name. She woke up immediately, and I said, "Ruby, do you know who this is?" She said, "Yes, its Ron. Is Russ with you?" I said, "Yes, he's on the other side of the bed." She forced a smile, and said, "Thank you for coming," as she took his hand also. I said, "Thank you for waiting." With a surprised look on her face, the nurse went back to her station.

Several family members were there, and after Russ and I had visited with Ruby a few minutes we saw she was really tired, and we let her go back to sleep while we went over and visited with the family. Our second oldest sister, Garnet, who was from Arizona, said she had flown in and had been there with Ruby for the past three days. She said the doctors said they were surprised she was holding on so long, and she told them, "She's waiting for the boys. My brothers are on their way."

We visited for about half an hour and every time one of us spoke a bit loud, Ruby would stir and groan. I told the family she was subconsciously recognizing a familiar voice and was trying to respond to it. I told the family that since we were the last ones coming, and everyone had visited with her, I was going to go wake her up and pray that the Lord would take her home quickly and painlessly. They agreed to that, and we all gathered around Ruby's bed.

I took her hand, and she woke up. I said, "Sis, I'm going to pray for the Lord to take you home out of this pain, and into glory." She squeezed my hand and said, "Please do." We joined hands and I prayed a simple prayer, asking God to take her home quickly and painlessly. We finished and went back to our chairs while Ruby went back to sleep.

About forty-five minutes later Ruby said, "What? Let go? Yes, I want to let it go." There was a brief pause as I motioned for all the family to stay quiet. After the brief pause Ruby said, "Yes, I'm letting go." She pushed herself up on her left elbow and reached up toward the corner of the room, saying, "I'm coming," then laid back on the pillow and was gone. I checked her vital signs and she had none. I called the nurse, and when she arrived, I told her my sister had just gone to be with the Lord.

Her response was somewhat sarcastic as she said, "How can you determine someone's death? Are you a doctor, or something?" I said, "No, I'm not a doctor, but I've been a surgical tech for twenty-four years, with one year in Vietnam. I know how to check vital signs, and I know that when someone doesn't have any, they are gone. My sister doesn't have any."

She checked Ruby for vital signs and when she finished, she stepped back and said, "Well I'm sorry. You're right. Your sister is gone." I said, "I know I am right, and that my sister is gone, but I'm not sorry." She looked at me kind of funny and asked, "Why are you not sorry?"

I told her, "Look at my sister. She has lost over forty pounds since the last time I saw her at the end of July. She was locked up in a sick, painful body in complete misery. Her Lord and savior just came into this room and took her out of all that misery and into glory with Him. I wouldn't call her back if I could call her to the best moment of her life, because she is so much better off now."

The nurse looked at me and said, "I wish everyone felt that way when they lost a loved one." I simply told her that I wished everyone's loved that died was ready to meet the Lord as my sister was.

It has been thirty-two years (this September) since she went home with Jesus. The amazing thing is that I have had absolutely no remorse about her dying on that day, and I have never had any since that day. When she went, my mind went back to the last Sunday in July of 1973 when she and her family came out to California on a vacation trip.

They came to our Church on that last Sunday of July. Ruby had been actively involved in an old, traditional Lutheran church for fourteen years. That Sunday I preached a message out of the Book of Joel entitled "Multitudes In The Valley Of Decision." I gave the altar invitation and Ruby stepped into the aisle and came to the altar. As she knelt down, I knelt beside her, and asked, "Can I help you, Sis?" She said, "Yes, I want to receive Jesus as my savior. I have been in Church for fourteen years but have never been saved."

We prayed and she was wonderfully saved. She went home, resigned that Church, and got involved in a Bible believing, Christ loving, salvation preaching church and served Jesus faithfully until she got the cancer that He used to take her home with. That's why I had, and have, no remorse. Ruby didn't die, she just moved. Instead of her address being in Lincoln, Nebraska, it is now in Eternal Heaven. She is out of all the pain and sorrow and the miseries of a terrible marriage relationship that she was bound in (as Revelation 21:4 states) and is in eternal glory with Jesus. What is there to be sorrowful about? Every time I think of her passing away on September 1, 1988, I am reminded of the awesome privilege of leading her to Jesus on the last Sunday of July in 1973.

After the time I was back there her son Terry called and asked me, "Uncle Ron, why do you think God took my Mother, especially after He healed her from a different type of cancer just two months earlier.?"

I said I didn't know for sure, but if he really wanted my opinion, I would give it. He said he did, and I said, "In Isaiah 57:1 the Bible says, "The righteous perisheth (dies), and no man layeth it to heart: and merciful men are taken away, none considering that the righteous is taken away from the evil to come." I told him that means God sometimes takes the righteous out of this world to avoid something evil that would be in their future, that they may not have the faith to deal with.

I told him I had thought and prayed much about it, and I believe God took her out of the mess she had lived in with Grover, her husband, for over thirty years. I told him I didn't like to talk ill about his dad, but after he had viciously and obscenely rejected his promises, and everything Ruby believed in, after the first cancer was cured; I believe God just took her out of the misery and took her home.

He was quiet for a time, then he said, "Uncle Ron, that's exactly what I believe. I just didn't have the scripture, and I didn't know how to put it into words. Don't feel bad about telling me because what you said is true. I know how dad was. I lived through it for years with mom, and I know how it affected her far more than me. I'm glad He took her." That closed the door on the subject. I heard Grover died two or three years later, living in a little travel trailer beside his sister's house. They said he died screaming and cursing, and out of his head. I am so thankful that she didn't live to see it.

So, cancer lost another battle. God used it as a positive tool to deliver Ruby; and to show the extended family that Heaven is real. It was a definite confirmation when she reached towards the ceiling, said, "I'm coming!" and left. To me, that again proves beyond doubt that God is truly God and... *cancer is JUST cancer... ...*

THE PROMISE IN THE MIDST OF CANCER

The next attack by cancer came in early 1988. We were informed that Arlee's mother Erma was diagnosed with cancer of the kidney, and it had metastasized to other parts of the body. It was stage four, and terminal.

We drove from Billings to Livingston and back several times to visit her. We had a small daycare at the Church, which was helping to pay the church bills, especially the mortgage payments. Arlee and her sister, Bonnie, ran the daycare.

After we had driven over to visit Erma several times, Bonnie took a week off and spent it with Erma. Arlee and I were coming home one Saturday afternoon, and as we were quietly driving, I noticed Arlee was silently crying. She very seldom cries, and I asked her why she was crying then.

She said, "Oh, honey, I wish I could come over and spend a week with my Mother, but I can't." I asked her why not, and she said it was because of the daycare. I said, "No, honey, you can come spend a week with your mom week after next."

She objected and said she couldn't because there was no one else to run the daycare if she wasn't there. I told her I was going to inform the parents the coming week and close the daycare on Friday evening so she could go be with her mother the week following.

Arlee objected because it would be eliminating the income for the Church. I told her God would provide for the Church in some way that would not deprive her of spending time with her mother. She thanked me and told me she was very thankful for that.

Suddenly I saw an amazing phenomenon and said, "Honey, look at that rainbow." It had been raining for some time and the rainbow had been visible for quite a while. She said, "What about it?" I pointed out that one end of the rainbow was on the roadway bank, while the other end was on the railroad track paralleling the highway. The entire rainbow was only about a thousand feet long and we could see the vegetation growth at both ends of the rainbow. It followed us for about five miles as we drove along.

The fact of it moving with us as we drove was no phenomenon because the rainbow appears because of the way the sun shines through the raindrop crystals so it would continue to be seen from wherever it was observed. The phenomenal thing about it was how short, bright, and transparent it was. Arlee and I discussed that for some time as we drove along.

I asked her if she remembered what the rainbow was, and she assured me that she did, which I knew she did, of course. I just wanted to get her to talk a bit so it would get her mind off of her grief about her mother's situation.

We both well know that the rainbow was God's sign, or symbol, to man that He would never again destroy the world by a flood. The story is found in Genesis, chapter nine, Where God says in verse 13, "I do set my bow in the cloud, and it shall be for a token of a covenant between me and the earth." He goes on in verses 14-16 saying that He is doing that as an everlasting covenant between Him and man that the earth shall never again be destroyed by a flood.

Does that mean the earth will never be destroyed again? Oh, no! Not by any stretch of the imagination. In fact, there are several places in the Bible where God tells us He is going to destroy this world when Jesus comes back in Judgement. One of the clearest places He tells us this is in II Peter, chapter three, verses ten through twelve where we are told He will destroy the world the second time by fire. In fact, He specifies it will be with fervent heat, and that it shall all be dissolved. But that is another story altogether.

Coming back to our trip home from seeing Arlee's mother, I told her, "Honey, there's no way of proving it, but I personally think God showed us this little, beautiful rainbow, such as we have never seen before, for a special reason." She said, "Really? What reason would that be?" I said, "Well, I'm not sure about it, but because the rainbow was so short that we could see both ends of it, and because it was so bright and brilliant, I believe God showed it to us personally. I believe He was reminding us that His promises are not something just in general; but are rather very specific."

Arlee's mother passed away a few weeks later on December 15, 1989. Yes, Arlee did go and spend the week with her mom. It was one of the greatest gifts I could have ever given her, and I wouldn't have begrudged her that time for anything. We did close the daycare, giving both Arlee and Bonnie time with her before she went. Of course, there was sorrow over her going, but after seeing that rainbow, and discussing it, Arlee never had any real problem with her mom's passing.

Of course, we both remembered the first time she had cancer, and we came up to see her. We remembered having the wonderful opportunity to lead her to Jesus, and cancer could never take that away. God's power and presence are supreme and sovereign; abiding with us eternally, and cancer, well, … *it's JUUST cancer…* And is one day going to do just like all the other evils in this world. It is going to pass away and never be remembered again. The person who puts their faith in Jesus, however, is going to live in joy eternally.

One of the biggest problems with cancer that causes people so much trouble is the *fear* that comes with the diagnosis. When the doctor tells a person "You have cancer," many people think that is a death sentence automatically. Some time it is, but more often it is not. It depends on a lot of variable things. Things such as "What kind of cancer is it?" "How long have you had it?" "What stage is it?" and many other factors.

The problem is when the clutches of fear grab ahold of a person, it often time incapacitates their ability to think, act, or feel anything other than the fear. When that happens, they almost stop any kind of a normal life. At least until they can make an adjustment to it.

What compounds a situation that makes it almost unbearable for some people, is the hopelessness that often engulfs a person because of the helplessness they feel. They get into an emotional quagmire because of the fear and all of their "instinctive reasoning" is focused on what they fear is to be the inevitable result.

Thank God that most people, Christian and non-Christian alike, usually are able to work themselves out of that numbing reaction to the "bad news." It may take a lot more time for some than for others; but the door is open, and the path well-traveled, for them to continue on with a productive, happy, and fulfilling life.

THE "WAKE UP" OF CANCER

One of the very first things one needs to realize is that ...*it is JUST cancer* ....which is not said, or meant, in any way to trivialize cancer. Someone will respond by saying, "Yes, but cancer will kill you!" That, however, is only partly true. Let us agree that cancer will kill you, of course. Cancer, however, is like any other potentially deadly disease. It is like heart disease (the #1 killer in America according to reports), or like diabetes, or renal (kidney) failure, or like emphysema, or Covid 19, the flu, or so many more.

Very few people, however, interpret these other diseases as "positive and imminent death sentences." They realize they have something that is basically terminal, eventually, and they begin to focus on how they can make the life they have left (however long that may be) become a truly productive and enjoyable life. But then, isn't that what we all should be doing, all of the time, in our current lives, whatever they are like?

Why should anyone be content, or resigned, to such a mediocre, neutralized, meaningless life that they would need a "negative diagnosis" of any kind to prompt and stimulate them to realize the value of life; and to motivate them to "wake up" and begin to really live that life, rather than just continue to exist through it. We need to be realistic about life, and the brevity of it. The Psalmist says in Psalm 103:15-16, "As for man, his days are as grass: as a flower of the field so he flourisheth. For as the wind passeth over it, and it is gone; and the place thereof shall know it no more."

That's what life is like. Like the grass that springs up, grows for a short while, withers, and dies, so is man in comparison to eternity. Here for a moment, then gone. The question we must face is *"What shall we do to prepare for the eventuality?"*

The person who gets a diagnosis of cancer, or any other potentially terminal disease, has a "wake up call" to alert them to the problem. It also gives them time to plan what they are going to do about the problem. Another benefit is that it alerts them to the need to make the remaining time they have left meaningful for family, friends, and themselves.

But, what about the person whose car misses the sharp curve? Or the one who experiences their car, or an oncoming one, crossing the yellow line? Their life is terminated immediately with no "wake up" call to enable them to make what time is remaining of any value.

So, what is my point in speaking about dying instantly as opposed to dying slowly by something like cancer? It is simply this. When a person dies instantly, like in a car accident, all choice is taken out of their hands. There is no chance to make some kind of decision about preparing for it in the time left because there is no time left. There is no choice because there is no time.

So, there can be many things worse than a diagnosis of cancer. Even if it is stage four terminal cancer. Any "sudden death" is worse for the person dying than death by cancer (or anything else) that is "long term," *if they are not a true Christian.*

If they are a true Christian the "sudden death" experiences is a blessing to *them* for the Word of God says in II Corinthians 5:8, "We are confident, I say, and willing to be *absent from the body, and to be present with the Lord."* That means as soon as they die, their soul is in the presence of Jesus in glory.

There is a "flip side" to that, however. It also means that if a person is not a true Christian, the moment they die their soul is in eternal torment in hell. God's Word also says in Luke 16:22d-23b, "The rich man also died, and was buried; and in Hell he lifts up his eyes, being in torment," so we need to realize that death is the end of the physical life, and the beginning of eternity, either in Heaven or Hell.

There is something else we need to realize, and that is what "true Christian" really means. Many people know about God and Jesus, but *they don't know God and Jesus! They know with the head, but not with the heart.* They are the ones God speaks to in James 2:19 when He says, "Thou believest that there is one God, thou doest well: the devils (demons) also believe and tremble."

Now we know the demons are not saved, and never can be. So, the "belief" James is talking about cannot be the heart belief God speaks of in Romans 10:9-10. There He says, "For with the heart man believeth unto righteousness: and with the mouth confession is made unto salvation."

It is the "heart belief, through faith, that saves a person. The "head belief" that is through man's reasoning and understanding does nothing but deceive a person. It is Religion, which is deceptive, devilish, and deadly, while the heart belief is a Relationship with God, through Jesus Christ as Savior. It is healing, heavenly, and honoring to God.

That is why I speak of a death by cancer being better than an instant death because of the extra time the cancer patient has. It gives them time, if they are sincere Christians, to interact with family, friends, medical personnel, and perhaps others, in order to share their faith with them.

If the person is not a Christian, it is even more important, perhaps, because during that time someone may minister to them in some way through which they could be saved. That would be well worth the wait because they would have been delivered from a Godless eternity of pain and sorrow and into a blessed eternity of joy and peace with God.

If you are not a true Christian as you are reading this, you really should become one. A person can become a true, or genuine, Christian through a brief, but sincere process of obeying Gods Word, and accepting Jesus Christ as Savior by faith. All it involves is a *simple, but sincere prayer.* You can pray these words, or some like them, as long as they sincerely come from your heart.

"Dear God, I know that I am lost, and am a sinner. I know I cannot save myself from an eternal punishment for sin. I ask you to forgive me for all my sin. Lord Jesus, I ask you to come into my heart and life and be my Savor. I ask it in Jesus' name, Amen."

If you will sincerely pray this prayer the Bible says that you are saved, or "born again." This is what God was speaking of in Romans 10:9-10 when He said, "That if thou shalt confess with thy mouth the Lord Jesus, and shalt believe in thine heart that God hath raised Him from the dead, *thou shalt be saved.* For with the heart man believeth unto righteousness; and with the mouth confession is made unto salvation." That is a profession of faith that enables a person to become a true Christian and have a real relationship with God through faith in Jesus Christ as Savior.

If you will not repent of your sins (sincerely pray for forgiveness and turn from them), you can never be saved, and you have nothing left ahead of you except death and eternal punishment. What a terrible tragedy this is, especially when God has done so much in order to save us, and all we need to do is receive it in faith.

THE LIES OF SATAN

Satan deceives many people through procrastination. He lies to them when they begin to feel guilty as God speaks to their heart about their sin, and tells them something like this: "You don't have to worry about all that. You *have plenty of time to deal with those issues.*"

Many people will quickly respond to his lies because they don't like feeling guilty, and they don't want to think about changing their lives. So, they often put it off until they find out it is too late. By that time, they have been putting God off for so long that He may not continue to deal with them. That is tragic for they have lost their opportunity to ever be able to go to Heaven because of unrepented sin.

Another lie Satan puts in people's mind is this: "If you get saved, you will lose so much. You will have to give up what you have, and what you are doing for a dull and drab life of going to Church." That certainly is a lie, and common reasoning definitely proves it.

The Bible says that God loved the world so much that He gave His only begotten (born) son to die on the cross for man's sins. Do you think He would do so for such a shallow purpose as to deprive you of all that is good, meaningful, and worthwhile?

How ridiculous and senseless an idea like that is. God would never even consider that idea because even considering it would be foolish. So, what is the truth concerning being saved? The truth about being saved is that it is the greatest thing that God ever did concerning man. It was an act of supreme love and sacrifice on God's part, in order to rescue and bless mankind who were totally and completely unworthy and sinful.

That being true, how foolish, and totally unthinkable it would be to even consider the lying excuses Satan tries to deceive the minds, of those who need God's love and mercy so much, with. Yet so many people subject themselves to those excuses rather than just accepting God's free grace.

Don't believe the devil's lies. God doesn't want to deprive you of anything of any lasting, or eternal, value. He wants to forgive you of your sins and give you a life where He, and all that will bless you, outshines everything the world has to offer.

If you are a Christian, God is not punishing you, or treating you badly, with a diagnosis of cancer. He is using it to awaken you to the time you have left, to be a witness to those who are not Christians, whether they are in your family, or not. In ways far beyond our understanding He is working His perfect will out for His glory and for our very best. Make the very best of your time and opportunities, and remember …..it is JUST cancer…..!

An older couple started coming to our Church in years gone by. Their names were Keith and Fran Kolszak. Keith's nick name was "Tuffy" because he had been a little guy all of his life and had a typical "little guy" attitude growing up. We got to be close friends, and I would go out on visitation afternoons or evenings to their house often. We would just sit and "chew the fat" as we passed the time away.

One day while I was there a fellow came by to talk to Tuffy about something. Tuffy (Keith) introduced him to me as his twin brother, Ken. We shook hands and Ken said he had to go. Before he left, I invited him to Church, thinking that since Tuffy and Fran were both consistent Christians attending our Church, Ken may be inclined to come and visit.

I found out I was wrong when he informed me that Church wasn't his thing, and he wasn't interested. I did not press the point, but I stopped by his house three or four times in the next few months. Besides that, Tuffy invited him several times, but each time Ken would give the same negative reply.

Some months after I had met Ken, I got a phone call from Tuffy one day. He said, "Pastor, I just wanted to let you know Ken is up here in St. Vincent's hospital, dying with cancer. The doctors said they didn't expect him to live through the night."

I told him I would be up there within a half hour. He said, "No pastor, you don't need to come up here. Ken is in a medical coma and is asleep. He wouldn't even be able to hear you." I said I would see him in a bit and hung up the phone. I told Arlee where I was going and asked her to keep me in prayer.

I arrived at the hospital a few minutes later and walked into the nurse's station where Tuffy and Fran were waiting. There was a young, arrogant doctor there doing some writing in a chart. I had worked with him several times and we didn't hit it off too well. He was pretty impressed with being "a doctor," and seemed to be pretty "full of himself," as the old folks used to say. I have just never been too impressed with positions and titles, and he knew that.

I asked Tuffy where Ken was, and he pointed at the room across the hall. He said, "He's still under the coma," and I told him I was going in and pray for him anyway. He told me alright, and I went to the door.

The young doctor spoke up in a smug way, and said, "It won't do any good. He is asleep in a coma and won't come out of it for quite some time." That all reminded me of the time I had gone in to see my sister in Lincoln, Nebraska some years before. I just smiled at him and said, "Well, we'll see," and went into the room.

I stepped into the room and closed the door, and when I did Ken was sitting up in bed looking at me. He said, "Hello, Pastor, how are you?" I gave him my usual answer and said, "I'm fine Ken but how are you?"

He looked at me, and with a little shrug said, "I guess I'm fine. The doctors have all told me about not having any time left. They don't expect me to live through the night." I went over to him, shook hands, and said, "Ken you know what you're facing. You are getting ready to take the longest journey any person can take. That is the journey into eternity; and I would like to tell you about my friend Jesus. He really would like to go with you through that journey, so you don't have to go it alone."

I like to use that particular approach, which I have used frequently with people in those circumstances. It is a very non-offensive approach to what is often a delicate subject with people. It also addresses the very fact that their mind is dwelling on in that condition.

Ken smiled at me and said, "Please do, Pastor." I pulled up a chair and opened my Bible and told him about Jesus. About ten minutes later we prayed, and Ken was a newborn child of God, headed for Heaven, and not Hell.

I told Ken he needed to share what he had just done with Tuffy and Fran and he smiled and said, "Call them in." I went out without opening the door wide enough for them to see him. Tuffy said, "How's he doing, Pastor?" I said, "Well, why don't you and Fran go in and ask him? He has something to tell you?

I looked around to see how the smug doctor was taking this, and he looked like he was about to have some kind of a "conniption fit" as the old folks used to say. Tuffy and Fran opened the door and Ken was sitting up in bed with a big smile. (I never saw him smile as much before, or after, that day.") He said, "Hey, I just prayed and received Jesus as my Savior and boy do I feel good."

I looked around again to see how the smug doctor was taking this, but he was gone. He must have been moving fast because he wasn't even in sight down the hallway. Maybe he was afraid I was going to talk to him about it. I don't know. I just had a short, quiet prayer thanking God for the amazing grace that reigns over all of man's predictions and wisdom, to God's glory.

Ken lived for a little over three months before he passed away. During that time, he was dismissed from the hospital to his home under hospice care. I visited him several times during that period, and we always had some sweet fellowship. He was very weak and couldn't get out of his house. His condition and circumstances reminded me of Audrey Dodson several years before. The last time I saw him alive was two days before he went. He told me he was not the least bit afraid of dying, and in fact, was looking forward to going to Heaven with Jesus.

He looked at me very seriously and said, "Pastor, I don't have many regrets as I look back over my life, because I know I am forgiven, and on my way to Heaven. There is only one regret I have. I really regret that I will never be able to go to your Church and hear you preach. I really would like to be able to do that just once before I go."

I told him not to let that bother him because we had an eternity ahead of us that we could share in Heaven. He smiled and agreed with me. I prayed with him and went home. Two days later Tuffy called and told me Ken had just passed away.

I just prayed and thanked God because I knew Ken was out of his pain, and misery, and was enjoying indescribable blessings in glory with Jesus. I just praise the Lord and rejoice in the fact that God chose and ordained me for such a privilege as winning people to Jesus, and being the "vehicle" that He could work through to change people's destinies from Hell to Heaven.

It is so great to know that God has called Christians to speak His word to people, and that it has the power to cleanse from sin, give eternal life, and replace sorrow and misery with joy and assurance. What about cancer? It is only able to cause physical death. It is also subject to the authority and power of God, and is a defeated enemy because after all, ...it is JUST cancer....!

ASSURANCE DURING CANCER

Dale Vanderberg was a very dear minister friend of mine. He pastored in California for years and while he was there, we met and became very close. He came down from the Fresno area and preached a revival for me in Bellflower, near North Long Beach, for a week during which he stayed with us. We had a chance to get very well acquainted during that time.

After some years in California, he moved to Blanchard, Oklahoma, where he started two Churches, and pastored them for some years. We continued to be good friends during that time, and he came all the way up to Billings, Montana to preach a week's revival for me. We went down through Blanchard and visited him and his wife Shirley when we took a trip back east to one of our national conventions.

I do not know when Dale was diagnosed with Leukemia (a cancer of the blood) because he never mentioned it. We found out when we went through there and stayed a couple days with them. He told me that he had leukemia, but that it had been in remission for about five years, and it was during that time when he had come up and preached the revival for me in Billings. He said it had come back and the doctors didn't think it looked too good.

He just smiled and made some kind of comment about it not looking bad for him at all. He was satisfied either way it went. He had perfect assurance of his relationship with his Lord and had no fear at all. That is the beautiful thing about being a true Christian! Knowing you are born into the family of God, and that neither life, nor death, can defeat the person who is depending on the Lord and His grace!

The amazing thing about knowing Dale, and especially when he had leukemia, was the great spirit he had through it all. He never complained about it, or the pain he was going through, or the fact that it took him out of his Church and into a hospital bed; and he constantly encouraged other people when they came to visit him. What a difference it is between someone who is facing pain and death with Christ, and someone who must face them alone. That is why it is imperative for every one of us to carefully take inventory of our lives and not neglect the most important thing in life or eternity. That is a personal relationship with the God of eternity through Jesus Christ the Lord!

The last time we saw Dale was in the hospital when we drove through his area again. He was smiling and talking, and as upbeat as if he was having some kind of "minor procedure." A short time after that Dale went home to his reward with Jesus.

His faith and trust in his Lord were what made the big difference. He proved that old saying true which says, "It isn't just the way a Christian lives that proves the quality of their faith, but also the way they die."

Dale lived in his faith well, and he died in his faith well, because he well knew the physical death is not the end for the faithful Christian. It is just a transition to the fulness of life in glory with God, never to experience pain or death again. What a glorious promise, and assurance, genuine faith in Jesus Christ as Lord and Savior gives to the person who is facing the end of this physical life, and the beginning of the eternity they cannot see. The question again begs to be answered, "Do you have that assurance for yourself today?"

Nothing can deprive a faithful Christian from experiencing that because it is God's reward for living our faith in this world. Nothing can stop the joy of that experience, nor even diminish it, not even cancer. The reason for that, once again, is because …..it is JUST cancer…. and Jesus Christ is still Lord, God, and Savior for all time and eternity.

Cancer, like many other problems of the flesh (especially other diseases), is a formidable foe that continues to raise its ugly head and attack time after time. Sometimes with a family, other times with an individual, but the attacks go on, and so must the battle against them. It came back to our personal family.

Arlee's sister Bonnie had been a smoker for almost her entire life. She started smoking when she was nine years old, literally. I know that sounds almost impossible, but it is true. She smoked without the knowledge of her parents, of course, until she was in her early teens from what she told me. When most people who smoke, began to smoke in their lives, Bonnie was already a hard and fast consistent smoker at that age.

It was in 1993 or early 1994 when Bonnie was diagnosed with COPD, and the doctor said it was an advanced case. She got very weak and sick from it and looked like she was going to die very soon. She got to the point where she couldn't take care of herself, and with her husband working, he couldn't take care of her, either.

I asked Arlee if she wanted to bring Bonnie into our home and take care of her. She said she would really like to do so with one reservation. She said, "When it gets time for her to go, I want us to find her a care facility to live in because I don't want my sister to die in my house. I don't think I would ever be able to go back into the room she died in."

I agreed to that, and we talked to Bonnie about it. She was very agreeable to the suggestion, and very appreciative for it, so we moved her in with us, and she lived for sixteen months, during which several things happened.

One of the rules we have always had in our home since we became Christians is that if we ever agree to let anyone live with us on an extended basis, they must abide by the rules of our home, whether they agree with them, or not. The only other option is if they haven't moved in yet, don't! And if they are living here and decide they don't like the rules, then they must get packed and move. There is no "third option," or "plan B."

One of those rules is they must be willing to go to Church with us. Bonnie agreed to the house rules, including the one concerning Church, and so we moved her in. I moved my study from the room across the hall from our bedroom to a room in the basement. We moved Bonnie into the room across from us so we could keep a closer eye on her, especially at night. She left her door open a crack, and when Arlee or I would get up to go to the bathroom, we would check and make sure she was alright.

She lived with us for about six months or so, going to Church with us every service. One Sunday morning God really blessed. I preached a message (I don't recall what I preached on since it has been so long ago) and when I gave the altar invitation, Bonnie stepped out and came forward. When she knelt at the altar, I knelt beside her and asked if I could help her.

She said, "Yes, Ron. I have been backslidden for many years, and not serving the Lord. Living with you and Arlee has shown me what a Christian life should be. I want to rededicate my life to Jesus and get back where I should be with God."

We prayed and she repented for her sins and was wonderfully forgiven. She finished and we stood up, then she gave a public testimony that she had been backslidden and had just rededicated her life to Christ. I was, and still am, so thankful for God's faithfulness as He said in I John 1:9, "If we confess our sins, He is faithful and just to forgive us our sins and cleanse us from all unrighteousness." What a grand promise that is.

What about you? Do you have something in your life that you know you need to confess to God and repent for? You may know you have been saved, and perhaps you were actively and joyfully serving the Lord at that time, but that time is gone. You have perhaps been carrying a burden of sin about something and you have had a hard struggle with it. *If that is your case,* why not just stop and sincerely confess it to God and repent of it? You will be so glad you did, just like Bonnie was.

Bonnie came home from a doctor appointment about two months after she had rededicated her life and told me the doctor said he may need to put her on oxygen. I said, "Bonnie, if the doctor does put you on oxygen, you will only have two choices concerning your living arrangements. You will either have to quit smoking immediately, or we will have to find an extended living home for you." I went on and explained to her, "I am not trying to kick you out, for we love having you here," which we truly did.

I said, "Statistically the danger of fire increases 300% in a home when someone is put on oxygen because everything in the house gets saturated with oxygen and becomes extremely flammable. Arlee and I have worked very hard for a long time, and we don't want to take a chance on losing it all."

She said, "O.K., Ron. If the doctors put me on oxygen, I know I have that decision to make." A couple weeks or so later she came back from the doctor and told me the doctor was putting her on Oxygen the following week as soon as they got the equipment ready. I acknowledged it, and we left it at that.

That evening she asked Arlee if she would go out and sit with her on the porch while she had a cigarette. (We never allowed anyone to smoke in our house since we became Christians in June of 1968 either. Another of our rules.)

Later, Arlee told me they went out and sat on the porch and Bonnie told her about my discussion with her concerning her only two options. Bonnie said, "I wanted you to come with me as I smoked my last cigarette." Arlee asked her if she was out of cigarettes, and Bonnie said, "No, I've got about half a pack left, but I'm throwing them away. I am going to quit smoking because I love living with you and Ron, and I'm not going to do anything to jeopardize you or your home."

Bonnie never smoked another one for the rest of her life. She threw the remainder of the pack away, and later she told me she had prayed about it and the amazing thing was she was never bothered with even a desire to smoke after that. She told me she never believed she could ever quit smoking, so she never really tried to. She said she really wished she would have because smoking caused more trouble in her marriage than anything else she ever did.

It was about this time when she came home from the doctor and said he had discovered a lump in one of her lungs. I was really concerned about that and got her an appointment to see one of the surgeons I worked with. She went to see him and later he talked with me at work.

He said, "Ron, I've examined your wife's sister Bonnie, and she has a tumor in one of her lungs. It's not too big, yet, and it is in a good place for surgery to take it out. You've helped me on several of the same kind of surgeries, and it would only take about an hour and a half for the entire thing. We would just go in between the ribs and do a "wedge resection" and that would do it." (A wedge resection is the removal of a wedge-shaped piece of the lung with the tumor in it.)

I asked him when we could schedule her and have it done. He looked at me and said, "That's just it, Ron, we can't." He went on and told me why. A person must have one full liter of oxygen exchange (intake and output) per minute in order to come off the machine they use for anesthesia to put a patient to sleep and maintain their life while they are asleep having the operation.

He said Bonnie, in her deteriorated condition of C.O.P.D., which is a very serios lung disease, (literally caused by her extensive smoking) was existing on one fourth of a liter of exchange, even using an oxygen machine for everyday breathing.

He told me that if she was ever put to sleep with anesthesia, she would adjust to the full liter of oxygen produced by the machine breathing for her, and she would never be able to come off the machine and wake up. He then said he had that diagnosis confirmed by two of his surgical partners.

He had to explain that to Bonnie and the family and let them know that there was no more that could be done for Bonnie. The irony of the whole situation was that it would have been a fairly simple surgery, but the pre-existing damage to the lungs was beyond repair, and beyond help; and so, we all had to accept the inevitable.

Arlee came to me, and after praying about it, she said, "Ron, I've changed my mind about putting Bonnie in any care home. I want to keep her here in our home where I can love her and care for her through all of this."

Bonnie had never been much of a reader in her life. Before she had backslidden, she taught Sunday School for a period of time, and she diligently read her lessons and the Bible while she was doing that. She hadn't done that for some time when she came to stay with us.

After she rededicated her life to Christ that all changed. I would get up during the night, as did Arlee, to go to the bathroom and we would see Bonnie's door ajar and her light on. When we would peek in to be sure everything was okay, she would be sitting on the bed in her pajamas reading the Bible. She did that into the wee hours of the morning, night after night.

I talked to her about it one day and she said, "Ron, since I rededicated my life to the Lord, I have had a real hunger to read the Bible. More than any other time in my life." I told her what Jesus said in Matthew 5:6, "Blessed are they which do hunger and thirst after righteousness: for they shall be filled."

Bonnie lived with us for a total of about sixteen months, the last couple of which we had hospice come in and care for her also. On the last evening she was in her bed and some of the family was sitting in the dining room when we heard a "thump," and we heard Bonnie yell.

We ran to her room and found her on the floor in front of the bed. I went in and lifted her back into bed and asked what had happened. She said she had gotten up and went to the bathroom and when she tried to get back into bed she slipped and fell.

She sat up in bed, gasping, and I put my arm around her shoulders and held her hands with my other hand. Arlee was standing beside her, holding her hands with me, and some of the kids were standing around the bed. I asked her what the problem was, and she looked at me, rather frightened, and said, "I can't breathe. I can't breathe." I hugged her a little and kissed her on the forehead, and said, "It's okay, Bonnie. It's your time to go home with Jesus, and we're all here with you."

Whatever fear had been there passed away and she looked around the bed at us and said, "Alright. I'll see you later." With that she was gone. I laid her back on her bed and called hospice and the nurse came over and handled everything from there.

While the nurse was on her way Arlee said, "Ron, I am so glad we didn't put her in a home. I'm so glad she was in our home. And we were able to take care of her." She smiled through her tears and said, "I wouldn't take a million dollars for what I just experienced in helping my sister go home." Knowing my wife. The way I do, I don't believe she exaggerated the value she placed on the experience by one penny!

It was sad that Bonnie passed away, and all of the pain and misery she went through before she went home, but that's the point I am trying to make. Her going was divinely delayed by God, and it not only gave her the time to repent and rededicate her life to Jesus, but also to live some months in loving fellowship with Him.

We thought it was well worth it, and so did she. She passed away on March sixth of 1996 at the young age of just 48 years old. There could have been so much more if she had made different choices. She died at the exact age her dad did, and of the very same disease caused by the very same thing.

If, per chance, someone reading this is in bondage to tobacco addiction, or any other type, you can be free if you will. Just take a moment and ask God to forgive you for the sin you are indulging in that is in the process of ruining your body, and that which may be ruining your soul. Then get into Christian fellowship, and if need be, Christian counselling and support, and see God change your life. You may ask how I know you can be freed from the addiction and set free, and the answer is simple. Because God said so, and God *can't lie.*

In John 8:31-32 Jesus said, "If ye continue in my word, then are ye my disciples indeed: and *ye shall know the truth, and the truth shall make you free."* Then in verse 36 He says, "If the Son therefore shall make you free, *ye shall be freed indeed."*

We can rest on that because it is a promise of Jesus, and Jesus is God. So, what about cancer? Well, Jesus is Lord and God and….cancer is JUST cancer….!

A few years after Bonnie passed away from cancer her second oldest sister Beverley was diagnosed with cancer. We didn't know much about it because she didn't live here in Billings. She lived about a hundred miles east and we didn't get many visits from her.

A while later we got word that Beverley was in the hospital in Billings with stage 4 cancer. I believe it was kidney cancer. It wasn't long before she passed away. I never had the opportunity to talk to her about the Lord while she was in the hospital because there were a couple family members who were very hostile to the gospel, which was very unfortunate. I pray God's grace will reach them before their time to go.

Bonnie passed away in 1996 and Beverley passed away about five years later. Between their passing, however, cancer attacked our immediate family once again. God, in His merciful grace, worked miraculously through that attack, however.

In October of 1999 Arlee, her oldest sister Donna, and I were coming home from the hospital where I worked. Arlee was driving and I was in the front passenger seat, with Donna in the back seat. We were driving a little Buick Skylark, which is one of the low built, medium compact cars.

A full-size jeep came through the stop sign and T-boned us on the driver's door doing about forty miles per hour. It hit us so hard it pushed the driver's door completely in against the steering wheel. The driver was a young guy who played on the city hockey team, and evidently thought himself invincible. He told the officer he was "preoccupied" and didn't even see the stop sign, so he didn't even touch his brakes.

He hit us so hard that it didn't even skid us; it just flipped us over on our top and we slid across the intersection, hit the opposite curb, and slid down it about thirty feet where we came to a rest on our top. From the time we got hit to the time we stopped on our top everything went into "slow motion." I had heard people talk about going into slow motion during a crisis, but I never gave any credence to it; until it happened to me at that time, then I realized it was a very true and valid experience.

While we were tipping over, then sliding, and finally coming to a stop, I was totally calm and thinking of what I could do to help Arlee and Donna. Arlee was suspended in her seat belt, hanging upside down, and Donna was in the back seat crying and yelling Arlee's name, asking if she was alright.

I told Donna to quiet down, and that Arlee was unconscious and hanging upside down in her seat belt. The top of the car was so smashed in that I couldn't get past the console between the seats to try to help her, so I was going to need to get in the back seat and go out the window to try to help her.

I managed to slide between the front bucket seats into the back. Then I told Donna to turn her face and cover her head so she wouldn't be hit with broken glass. I kicked the window out, grabbed the metal edge, and slid out the window. I ran around to the driver's side and tried to reach Arlee. I could not reach her because of the car being so crushed down. All I had access to was her left hand and arm. I called her name and there was no response.

I checked her pulse eight times. Four times on the radial (wrist) pulse, and four times on the brachial (elbow) pulse. She had absolutely no pulse. At that time, I had been in medical work (surgery) for thirty-five years with four of them in the navy, and one of those as a corpsman in Vietnam. I could take a pulse on about anyone or anything, so I knew I was not missing her pulse. She had none!

After the eighth time I paused, and holding her hand, I prayed. I prayed a simple prayer and said, "Lord, please don't let her be dead. But if she is, I accept that, and I thank you for thirty-five years of a wonderful marriage. "(We had been married for the same amount of time that I was in medical work at that time.) I said, "I know you will give me the grace to get through this. In Jesus' name, amen."

I finished praying and got up and went around the car to see where the medical units were because I could hear the sirens. They told me they were coming down the street, so I went back to be with Arlee. I knelt beside the car and took her pulse again. It was a strong, bounding pulse. I took it another time and it was the same.

I prayed and thanked God she was alive. In my mind's eye I could see myself pushing her in a wheelchair for the rest of her life. I told the Lord I accepted that, as long as she was alive. (The awesome grace of God, however, is too great to be measured; and so, it was in this incident.)

I got down on my stomach, then I reached in and could just reach her chin. I touched her chin very carefully so I would not do any more damage to her neck if there was a problem with it. I spoke her name as I was touching her chin, and on the fourth time I called her name she groaned and asked, "What happened?" I told her we had been in a very serious accident, and I wanted her to stay awake and not to move because she could be hurt very badly. She acknowledged that and the next thing I felt was a paramedic tap me on the shoulder and tell me, "We've got this now, sir. Please step back." I backed out and updated them as to her apparent condition.

I have gone over the events of that night many times in my mind since then, and from the time we were hit to the time her pulse was restored was at the minimum six to eight minutes. I know people will raise their eyebrows at that because medically it is impossible for a person with a normal body temperature to be without a pulse for that length of time without suffering brain damage. The exception would be someone who had fallen into icy water, and drowned, and was resuscitated after much more than eight minutes without a pulse. I know, and I agree medically, but I also know by many different experiences that God can do anything, especially in answer to prayer. And in God's marvelous creation, the Spiritual always trumps the medical and physical.

Again, in the face of every doubt that may be expressed, I firmly believe my wife was dead, and that God raised her back to life in response to my prayer of complete surrender to His will. We need to remember that the Word of God teaches that a miracle must begin with an impossibility. If you can work it out some way naturally, it won't be a miracle. But God still works miracles, and our ministry is a living proof of that.

They got her out of the car and took her to the hospital I worked at (Billings Clinic) and she went into X-ray as soon as she was stabilized. She had a complete body scan for assessing her injuries. She had severe concussion to both sides of her brain, three fractured ribs, and three nondisplaced fractures of the pelvis. (Nondisplaced is where they are broken, but not out of natural alignment.) If they would have been displaced, they would have had to do a massive abdominal operation, go down to the floor of the pelvis, and stabilize them with metal plates and screws. Thank God, however, that we did not have to go through that. He is good, indeed.

During the body scan it was discovered that she had a large ovarian cyst on one of her ovaries. The doctor said we would need to reschedule her for elective surgery sometime in the near future when she got over the problem caused by the car wreck.

Two months later, the doctor operated on her on December 19th of 1999. After the surgery I talked with the surgeon. He said, "Ron I don't know if you will believe this, or not," then he smiled and said, "yes, out of everybody I know, I think you would be the first to believe it." I asked him what he was talking about.

He said, "Ron, that car wreck was a miracle of God in disguise. Because of it we took full body scans, and we found a large cyst on one ovary. We operated because of the cyst and found out *Arlee had cancer in both of her ovaries".* He went on to say, "This was confirmed by three different lab oncologists, and they said it was definitely cancer in both ovaries."

I knew what that meant. The usual life expectancy of someone with ovarian cancer is five years, with the last one being a hard one with Chemo and radiation. When that thought went through my mind, I said a quick, and sincere, prayer. I prayed, "Lord, thank you for the extra five years. She could have died in the accident."

Before I could say anything, the doctor went on and said, "Ron, the good news is that we believe we got it all, and that she is cancer free. The oncologists said it had not gotten out of the ovarian capsules, so it was completely contained within them."

He paused for a moment, then he added, "In all of our collective years of working with cancer we have never caught ovarian cancer this early. She should be completely free of cancer, but just in case, I am putting her on a five-year cancer follow up regimen with one of our oncology specialists."

We went through the five-year regimen, seeing the doctor twice a year for three years, then once a year for the last two. When we finished the last appointment, the doctor looked at us, and said, "Well, Arlee, you don't have to come back and see me again unless you just want to come by and say hello. You are totally cancer free, and your future looks great."

We were so grateful to God, and we still are. The 19th of December 2021 she was twenty-two years cancer free. That is a major miracle and was the talk of two large medical centers here in Billings for some time following. That was the reason God allowed us to go through that terrible car wreck, because it was the way He was revealing the cancer to us. That is also the reason I was able to pray that prayer of absolute surrender to God's will when I was kneeling beside that wrecked car and holding my unresponsive wife's hand while I prayed. I have learned (and I learned it before the wreck) how to trust God's will when it doesn't seem to make any sense or logic. He has a perfect plan for every one of us, and all that is needed is our faith.

Again, it was indeed a miracle of God, but is in no way limited to "special people," except for people of faith. That, in itself, does not mean that people who die of cancer, or any other disease, do not have faith. Many of them have great faith, but God in His wisdom and purpose has a reason for taking them.

In II Corinthians, chapter 12, Paul the Apostle had some kind of a physical problem, and he prayed three times for God to take it away. Paul said that God did not take it away but gave him the assurance that God's grace was sufficient for anything Paul needed to face. Paul's response was that God's strength was made perfect in Paul's weakness.

He went on to say, "most gladly will I therefore glory in my infirmities (for Christ's sake)." That should be the attitude of every Christian when they face problems, even cancer. The trouble is it takes a lot of spiritual growth to reach the point in life where one reaches the place that they will sincerely accept God's will, and know that His will is best for each, and everyone, of us ultimately.

I in no way claim to have matured spiritually to Paul's status; but I think that I have matured to the point of being able to know His will is best in every one of my situations. And, I have come to the point of trusting Him in those situations, though that is sometimes very difficult, and He must often deal with me repeatedly to get me to that point of surrender.

There have been many times, however, when I resisted His will, and pursued my own, to my detriment. It was often not that I didn't get "my way," which I often did; but it was without the blessings God wanted to give me at the time. I never received those blessings unless, and until, I came to the point of confessing my sin and pride, then He forgave and blessed me. If I didn't, He didn't.

By the time we reached the incident of the wreck and the discovery of the cancer with Arlee in 1999, I had been serving the Lord long enough to sincerely do what I knew I needed to do. When I did, He proved He was still the omnipotent (all-powerful) God Who could do anything, and cancer, well in comparison….it's JUST cancer….

A few years later (I don't recall just how many), I received a call from a niece who lived in Washington state. She said her dad, who was my older brother, had come down from northern Washington to live with her so she could care for him. She said he had cancer in both lungs and the doctor said it would be terminal because it was well advanced into stage four. I was very sorry to hear that the old nemesis was back once again. I also knew, however, that much of it was self-inflicted like it had been with Arlee's sister Bonnie.

Like her, Roland (my brother) had started smoking when he was about ten or twelve years old by sneaking around. He was a heavy smoker through his teens, and into his entire adult life. He had been a two to three pack a day smoker most of his adult life. He used to wake up in the morning coughing and the first thing he would do was to light a cigarette (while still in bed) and after he had inhaled three or four drags the coughing would stop and he could get up and go about his day. He did that literally for years.

I wrote him for about a year trying to get him to see his need for a personal relationship with the Lord. He was never really open to that and knowing I could never convince him against his own will I did not try to force the issue. I wanted the opportunity to have a personal one-on-one meeting with him so I could talk to him personally.

During the last year I called him three or four times and talked to him. He would listen a bit, then acknowledge that he understood what I was saying, but never made any response to it. When it was getting very close to the end, I flew out to Wenatchee and spent three days and nights with them. Roland was in terrible condition, having lost a massive amount of weight. He reminded me of how Ruby looked when I saw her the last time.

He had a peculiar routine that he went through every day. He would get up and go about his day until a certain time. I don't recall the exact time, but it was the same time every day. He had a cigarette rolling machine that he used to roll his own smokes. It was on the dash of his little pickup which sat in their driveway. Each day at the same time he would go out and sit in his pickup and roll twenty cigarettes at one time.

He would then smoke those cigarettes one after the other until they were gone. He would then roll six more cigarettes and smoke them. When he had finished them, he would say he was finished and go back into the house. He asked me if I would go out and sit with him while he smoked, and I agreed to as long as we could have the windows down. He agreed to that so we would go out and sit and visit while he did his routine.

The first day I sat with him I tried to get a conversation started about his spiritual needs. He looked at me with tears in his eyes and said, "Don't talk to me about that. When anyone talks to me about that, or about war, it scares me really bad. I don't want to hear about any of that stuff." So, we talked about other things that happened while we were growing up.

It was terrible for me to know he was dying and was so closed to the Gospel. It was very difficult to know that without Christ as Savior, he was doomed to endless eternity separated from God. It was heart breaking to know that was true about him, and about every other person in the world who rejects, or neglects, Jesus Christ as their personal Savior. But when people just close themselves to the Gospel there is nothing that can be done against their free moral choice.

What about you today? Do you know *for sure* your sins are forgiven and Jesus lives in your heart as your Savior and Lord? *Religion is never enough. We must have a personal, intimate relationship with Jesus Christ* as Savior and Lord, or face a Godless eternity with no help, and no hope. It is so tragic to realize the number of people who choose to neglect and reject eternal life for the temporary satisfaction of the flesh. For all eternity they will dearly regret the choices they made and the foolish emptiness of those choices.

All it takes is a simple, sincere prayer of repentance and commitment, such as this.

> *"Dear Lord God, I know that I am a sinner; and that I am lost. I believe Jesus is the only Savior for all mankind. I ask you to forgive me for my sins, and Lord Jesus, I ask you to come into my heart and life and be my Savior. Help me to live faithfully for you. I ask in Jesus' name. Amen!*

With that simple prayer the Bible says a person is passed from death to life if it is prayed sincerely. They are passed from condemnation to justification. From a destiny in Hell to an eternal destiny in Heaven. From being a child of the Devil (John 8:44) to being a child of God. We have God's promise on these things!

Now, some people may say, "Well, what else do I have to do?" That's the beauty of a true relationship with Jesus Christ as Savior. You don't have to do anything else to enter into that relationship. God has done everything else through the life, death, burial, and resurrection of Jesus Christ.

His sinless life made Him qualified to be acceptable as God's sacrifice for sin. His atoning death paid the price for that sin for every individual who will personally respond to His invitation by faith. His victorious resurrection shows He has power and authority over sin, death, the grave, and hell, for all time and eternity. It justifies every person who will come to Him in simple faith and not rely on anything they have done or can do. It is all of God!

God's grace was manifested in another life along about the same time Roland was going through his struggle. I received a strange call from a lady named Penny Whitaker. She asked, "Pastor, would you come and visit with me?" I politely asked her who she was, and she told me her name. I didn't recognize it, so I asked her if I knew her, or her me.

She told me we didn't know each other personally but she and her daughter (or daughters) had visited our church twice some years ago. I got her address and went to visit her. She usually had at least one of her daughters there with her, which makes it harder to talk with someone about their personal spiritual needs.

I was finally able to visit her when no one else was there. After talking with her about her spiritual needs, and what the Bible said about them, I had the opportunity to lead her to Christ in prayer. There was an immediate change in her entire manner. As the realization of what she had done truly registered on her, she relaxed and said she was no longer afraid or anxious. We visited a number of times after that and she seemed relaxed, unafraid, and content.

Penny passed away a few months after she had first called me. I was very thankful for the opportunity to get to know her and to minister to her. The greatest thing I am thankful for, however, is that I shall one day see her in Heaven.

So, you see, her having cancer, and even dying because of it, was not a bad thing after all. It turned out to be a blessing because she became aware of her own mortality and her needs that only God could meet. He met them for eternity and blessed her beyond her furthest imagination because He is the all-powerful, saving God; and cancer, well……it is JUST cancer….!

Along about this time we received a phone call from Arlee's youngest sister Terri's husband, Roger. He told us he had some bad news for us. He told us that Terri had bladder cancer five years before and had gone through treatment. The treatment had cleared her of all the cancer, and she didn't need to come back to see the doctor for at least five years.

Around Thanksgiving, about four and a half years after the doctor told her that, Roger said Terri started to have some serious pain. He took her to the doctor, and they did a complete examination which showed the cancer had come back.

The doctors told them "They could not do anything however,

because it was too late. They should have come in earlier. The cancer had metastasized to the liver and other areas." The x-ray of the liver showed it was almost covered with cancer Roger said.

We drove over to Clyde Park to see them, and she was bedridden and unable to get up. I was out in the yard visiting with Roger while Arlee was in the house with Terri. Arlee came out and told me Terri had said for Arlee to have everyone leave the house and for me to come in because she needed to talk to me.

I went into the house and pulled a chair up beside Teri's bed. I said, "Can I help you, hon? Arlee told me you wanted to talk to me alone." She said, "Yes, Ron, I do." She said there were three things that really bothered her. I gave her a moment to collect her thoughts, then asked her what those things were.

She said, "The first was trying to get my family to accept the fact that I was dying. They just wouldn't accept that and thought there was something the doctors could do like they did the first time. I finally got them to realize there wasn't anything left to do, and they finally accepted the fact."

She paused a bit, then said, "The second thing was me getting my mind around the fact that I wasn't going to be at my son's wedding, which is coming up in a couple of months. I finally accepted that, and he and I talked, and he finally accepted the fact also."

She paused a little while, then said, "The third thing is the biggest of them all, and the one that really scares me." I asked her what that was, and she paused again and, with tears in her eyes, she said, "I know I'm not ready to die because if I do, I will go to Hell, and that really scares me."

I took her by the hand, and said, "Terri, God loves you so very much that He gave His only Son to die on the cross for your sins, and for mine. You don't want to go to hell, but He doesn't want you to go to Hell even more. He wants you to go to Heaven because that will make the sacrifice which Jesus made for you on the cross really meaningful for you personally."

I went on and told her, "Terri, God says in I John 1:9, "If we confess (repent) our sins, He is faithful and just to forgive us our sins, and to cleanse us from all unrighteousness." That means God will take away all of our sins and we will be made worthy to go to Heaven. You can do that by a simple prayer if you are willing to pray with me right now."

She said she would really like to do that, so I led her in a sinner's prayer simply asking God to forgive her for her sins and asking Jesus to come into her heart. It took about two minutes, and the sins were gone, and she was a new child of God.

She looked at me, wiped the tears from her eyes, and said, "Thank you so much, Ron. I am no longer afraid of dying, and I know I am going to Heaven." Her whole countenance was changed, and it was clearly evident that her life had done so, too. She asked me if I would go out and send Roger in so she could tell him. I did, and he was really happy and relieved when she shared her decisions with him.

We visited a while longer, then drove home that Friday evening, talking about how good and gracious God was. Arlee was so happy she could hardly talk because she had been instrumental in helping both of her younger sisters be assured Heaven as their eternal home.

On Monday morning at 10:00 A.M. the phone rang. I answered it and it was Roger. He said, "Ron, Terri just passed away at 9:00 this morning. She went peacefully, and I want to thank you and Arlee for coming over to see her Friday." I simply told him that it was our privilege and pleasure to do so.

She had a nice funeral service, which was actually a "graduation service" to celebrate her graduating from this life to glory. I didn't have the opportunity to preach the service so I could not explain the difference. There is a great difference, however, for a Christian never really dies. Their body dies but their soul simply transitions to glory. However, that is not true for the unsaved person who is not a Christian. Their body dies, and their soul transitions to Hell for eternity. I know there are many people who say they don't believe in Hell, but that is really foolish thinking. In essence, it is calling God a liar because He spoke of Hell multiple times to try to warn people away from it.

In fact, Jesus tells a story in Luke 16:19-31 about two men. One was a rich man who didn't believe in God and had no faith. The other was a poor man who had nothing but faith. Jesus said in verse 22-24, "and it came to pass, that the beggar died, and was carried by the angels into Abraham's bosom (Heaven): the rich man also died, and was buried, and in Hell he lift up his eyes, being in torments, and seeth Abraham afar off, and Lazarus (the beggar) in his bossom. And he cried and said, Father Abraham, have mercy on me, and send Lazarus, that he may dip the tip of his finger in water, and cool my tongue; *for I am tormented in this flame.*" That is the fate of every person who dies without knowing Jesus as Savior.

On the other hand, Jesus speaks to Martha about her brother Lazarus (a different man with the same name), who believed in Jesus as Savior, and who had just died. In John 11:25-26 Jesus said, "I am the resurrection and the life: he that believeth in me, though he were dead, yet shall he live. And whosoever liveth and believeth in me shall never die. Believeth thou this?" Martha's answer was, "Yea, Lord: I believe that thou art the Christ (Savior) which should come into the world."

Jesus was not speaking of physical death for Lazarus was already dead physically. He was speaking of spiritual death which is the separation of the soul from God for eternity. That is the kind of death the rich man experienced in Luke 16, which Jesus talked about, who went to hell.

The beggar, whose name was Lazarus, (not Martha's brother) experienced spiritual life when he went to Heaven. That is the wonderful thing about being able to talk to someone and explain it to them. If they will believe, and receive Christ as Savior, it does literally change their eternity from Hell to Heaven. If they refuse to believe the Word, and refuse to receive Christ as Savior, they have willfully chosen their own fate for eternity, and the full responsibility is on them for their choice.

Terri was a perfect example of a person who experiences the worst, and the best, of life. The worst was to have cancer, which is a terrible disease, indeed, and not be able to look forward to going to Heaven. The cancer gave her pain, and took her physical life, which is only temporary. Her personal relationship with Jesus Christ, which was gained by praying and repenting, gave her peace and spiritual life which are eternal. That is why it is so important to know Jesus as Lord. Why? Because Jesus is God, and…….cancer is JUST cancer……!

REJECTION DURING CANCER

Arlee had an older brother named Richard. He and I were good friends when I was not saved and was leading a rather tough life. When I committed my life to Christ Richard's attitude cooled toward me quite noticeably, but we were still friendly with each other. When I went into the ministry, and became a Pastor, it was almost as if I had done him some kind of a personal wrong.

His attitude became openly hostile towards me though I had never wronged him. He lived in Washington state, and we lived in California. Then we moved to Montana but there was still no communication with him. We saw him a couple of times when he came back to Montana to visit some relatives, but it was very brief. When we saw him, I spoke to him but all he did was glare at me and walk on by with not so much as one word.

A few years later we heard that he was diagnosed with throat cancer. Arlee said she would really like to go to Washington and see him. I told her to call him and see when he would be home, and I would be glad to drive her out to see him.

She called him and told him we wanted to come out so she could see him, and he very sarcastically told her, "You are welcome any time you want to come; but Ron Palmer is not welcome anywhere near my place at any time." She knew I had never done anything wrong to him, so her reply was. "Anywhere my husband is not welcome I don't want to be there." He said, "Fine," and that ended the conversation.

He and his wife got divorced after fifty years of marriage. He moved back to Montana, and after a few years he married an old girlfriend. A few years later she died, and he continued living in their home. One of his two daughters lived close to him, and they spent a lot of time together.

I was glad of that because a couple years or so after his second wife's death Richard was diagnosed with cancer again. I don't know what kind it was but after he had it for a while, he contacted Covid. His daughter took him into the hospital and a night or two later he died of the Covid.

That was another case like my older brother. They had multiple times when someone was willing to share the greatest truth in the world with them, but they spurned the opportunities and went into eternity the way they chose.

God's Word says, "My Spirit will not always strive with man." That means when God speaks to people over and over, there will come a time when He stops speaking to them, and allows them to go the way of their own choosing, even for eternity. How tragic to reject all of the love and grace that *God wants to give a person, then must be aware of their own rejection and what they will have to do without for all eternity.*

Some people feel, or think, that cancer, with all its disease and pain, is the worst thing a person could ever experience. That may be true for a Christian who has cancer for an extended period of time, then dies. However, what they receive when they enter into the actual presence of God, because of their faith, erases all memory of all that misery.

That, however, is not true for the lost person who has no faith in Christ. They may well feel that their pain and misery in this life is the worst thing they will ever experience, but that's not true. Many times, they just want to "die and be out of their misery," but that is not what happens. When they die without Christ they immediately go to Hell, just as the rich man in Luke 16 did.

When that happens that person has entered into misery which he never imagined, for all eternity, just like that rich man did. His cry was not a cry of achievement at getting out of his misery, but rather, one of horror as he cried out, "I am tormented in this flame." How could a loving God ever send any person to a horrible fate like that, in a horrible place like that, people often ask.

A loving God does not send a person to Hell. Their sins do! A loving God offers them saving grace, abundant mercy, and total and complete forgiveness for those sins, if they will repent of their sins and place their faith in Jesus Christ as Savior and Lord. If they will not do that (for whatever reason) then their sins send them to Hell which is the payment for all unrepented sins.

A loving God never sends a person to Hell, but unrepented sin always does. However, *a just God sees that sentence is carried out when grace and mercy are rejected through the rejection of Jesus Christ.* If He did not, He would be betraying His love, promise, and fairness to His only begotten Son. The Son who died that horrible death on the cross, in order to pay for those sins and provide that grace and mercy.

When people have the opportunity to hear the gospel and be saved, and they either neglect it or reject it, they are making two horribly tragic mistakes. First, they are rejecting everything God has done for them through His great love and grace. The second is that they are rejecting everything man (the Church) has done for them through prayer and evangelism.

That leaves the full responsibility for the choices they have made squarely upon themselves. God gives every person born into this world their free moral choice. That means they have the ability to not only make those choices, but to follow the course in life that they lead to, even if it is a tragic, eternal, self-destructive one.

Just think on that! Everything God has done through creating man, giving him the law by which sin is defined, by giving His only begotten Son by which the law was fulfilled, and man *could be redeemed, or saved;* all comes to naught for the person who rejects it. In addition to that tragedy, is the fact that everything man has done by establishing churches, preaching the gospel, evangelizing people who do not know God, creating all kinds of benevolent works that are helpful to their fellow man; all come to naught for that person who rejects man's efforts as well as God's.

If you are one of those people who have neglected, or rejected all of that, for whatever reason, please stop and think seriously about the consequences if you continue on the "journey of life" you are travelling. *No matter what you are seeking in life, there will never be anything worth comparing to what you will be giving up for eternity.* Please take a few moments while you are reading this and think seriously on what you are investing your life in, whether temporary or eternal. Life is so temporary and final, and when it's over there are no "seconds," or "make overs," *just the eternal results of the choices we have made.*

In view of that fact, it is amazing when we consider the wonderful opportunity God has given us. Through praying one sincere prayer (such as you have read in these previous pages) you can change your life, and your destiny, for eternity. If that sounds like "preaching," it really is meant to be. All the "preaching" in the world, however, is totally useless to the one who rejects it. God has given every one of us a "Free Will," or Free moral choice. With that free moral choice, however, comes the consequences for the choices made. We cannot escape those consequences no matter how much we would want to.

I served as a police chaplain for over fifteen years. I retired about six or seven years ago. It was a great time of service in many ways. One of those ways was by knowing, and serving with, the people I met during the years I spent.

One of those people was a Pastor by the name of Cliff. I didn't know him on a personal "close friend" basis, but as a close acquaintance. He was diagnosed with cancer, but again I didn't know the type. He often expressed his confidence that the Lord was going to heal him, much as my dear friend Pastor Joe did. We talked about it one day and Cliff said he didn't know if God was going to heal him or not, but he was satisfied either way it turned out.

He passed away after fighting cancer for about two years. During that time, however, he was able to faithfully make all his preparations for Church and family to carry on. He had a great funeral service and the officiating minister spoke exceptionally well of Cliff's life and the calm, confident way he embraced the fact of his coming death in this world, and the assurance of what he was looking forward to.

LIVING FOREVER EVEN THROUGH TERMINAL CANCER

That is the wonderful assurance every truly born-again Christian has from God. When you have committed your life to Jesus Christ as Savior, and you are faithfully serving Him as your Lord, you never die. Jesus said in John 11:25-26, "I am the resurrection and the life: he that believeth in me, though he were dead, yet shall he live: And whosoever liveth and believeth in me shall never die. Believest thou this?" *You see, the born-again Christian never dies because God gives them everlasting eternal life at the same time, they receive Jesus Christ as their personal Savior (are saved).* The body dies at the end of this worldly, fleshly life, but the soul of the righteous will never die. It immediately goes to Heaven to be with Jesus for all eternity. The Bible says in II Corinthians 5:6-8, "Therefore *we are always confident, knowing that, whilst we are at home in the body, we are absent from the Lord: (For we walk by faith, not by sight): We are confident, I say, and willing rather to be absent from the body and to be present with the Lord.*"

That is the status of the soul (the spiritual being) of the true Christian. When they are living in this world, *they are still separated from the glorious fulness of the presence of God by the flesh, even if they are faithfully walking with Jesus.* When they die physically the flesh dies, but the soul does not, as it goes to Heaven to be forever in the fulness of the glory of Jesus.

When the second coming of Jesus takes place, and time and life as we know it ends, the bodily resurrection of all people will take place. At that time everyone will receive a new body, Judgement will take place, and the righteous will go to Heaven with their glorified bodies. The unrighteous (unsaved) will go to Hell in the new body which shall never be destroyed.

The righteous will enjoy all the pleasures of Heaven that God has prepared for them for unending eternity. In like manner, the unrighteous will suffer all the miseries of Hell for eternity because they rejected God's grace and provision for them in their lives when they had the opportunity to make the choice.

I am not speaking of cancer from the perspective and standpoint of a non-involved spectator of the disease and its consequences. Nor from the standpoint of someone who is only aware of it through friends and close family. I am speaking from the perspective and standpoint of someone who has experienced the disease firsthand, and multiple times and types.

In 2018 my wife and I were sitting across the table from each other in our dining room. She looked at me in a strange way and said, "Honey, what is that growing in your eye?" I was surprised and had no idea of what she was speaking about. I asked her what she was speaking about, and she said, "You need to go in the bathroom and look at your eye. There is something fairly big growing there." I certainly did not need any more prompting, so I went into the bathroom and looked.

In my eye was some type of growth that I had never noticed before, even with all my shaving and looking at my face. I was surprised, and perplexed, because I had no notion of what it could be. It was about three quarters of an inch long, and about a quarter inch wide. It began on the white of my eye and was growing toward the pupil. It was just a little way from the pupil at the time.

I immediately called and got an appointment with the eye doctor at Billings Clinic. When I went in to see him a couple days later, he did a thorough eye exam on me. When he was finished, he said, "Well Ron, I don't have any idea what that is. I have never seen anything like it before. I would suggest you go see a specialist for this. There are none in Billings, but there is a very good one in Bozeman. I'll give you his office number and address." He did that and we left.

We went home and talked and prayed about it, asking for God's guidance. I told Arlee that since it was fall, I was really hesitant about going to Bozeman for treatment because it was going to be cold and snowy and muddy soon.

At the time I had a bunionectomy (removal of bunion) on my right foot and I was on crutches from it. I had no desire to be sloshing around in snow and mud, and driving a hundred and fifty miles each way over mountain passes and slick roads during bad weather. Arlee said, "Well what are we going to do? You sure can't just ignore it." I agreed with her and told her I was going to see our own doctor (Doctor James Threatt), whom we had known for years, and see if he had any ideas on what we should do.

We got an appointment and went to see him. He gave me a complete eye exam and when he was finished, he said, "Well Ron, I have been practicing my own eye service for over thirty-seven years, and I have never seen anything like this before in my life. I have no idea what it is. Maybe the best thing you could do would be to go on over to Bozeman and see that specialist. (I had told James about the referral.) Perhaps he could do something for it, or at least know what it is."

I asked him, (remember, we had prayed for God's guidance), if he could take whatever it was out and send it to the lab to have a pathologist examine it and hopefully identify it. He said he certainly could. He excised it (took it out) and sent it to the lab.

A week or so later I went in to see him again and he had the lab results back. He said it had been examined by three different pathologists and they had all examined it and agreed on what it was. It was a "non-differentiated squamous cell carcinoma (cancer), and the first one any of the pathologists had ever seen.

Dr. Threatt said he had called the eye research institute at Emory College in Atlanta, Georgia and talked to the professor that Dr. Threatt had taken his training under back in the early 70's. That same professor was now the director of the entire eye research department. When Dr. Threatt talked to him, he asked the professor if he had ever seen one of these before. The professor told him he had only seen six or seven of them in his entire career at Emory college. He asked Dr. Threatt to send him all of the information for him to confirm.

A couple weeks later he called Dr. Threatt back and confirmed the cancer diagnosis. He said the only treatment that was needed was to take enough tissue out around the cancer lesion to have "clear margins." He confirmed that Dr. Threatt had clear margins and all we needed to do now was keep watch on our annual check-ups to make sure nothing grew back. It has been five years, and everything is clear, thank the Lord Jesus for that.

Dr. Threatt said that kind of cancer would not metastasize to other areas of my body, but if it wasn't stopped it would consume my entire eye. Thank God it was removed and stopped, but then, why not? After all…. Cancer is JUST cancer…. and God is STILL God!

A year later, in 2019, I had a small rash on the left side of my forehead. I had it for about two or three years and it would not heal. I was suspicious of it, and I went to three different dermatologists for them to examine it. I saw them over a period of about two years, or so. Each of them looked at it very carefully and said it was nothing to worry about because it was probably just some type of heat rash.

I asked each of them if it could be cancer and they told me, "No, it isn't cancer. Maybe it's irritation from your hat band." I do wear a western (cowboy) hat as my major headgear, but I pointed out the fact that the rash was above the area where my hatband sat. Each of them, however, reassured me that it was not cancer.

It did not heal, however, and I remained very suspicious of it. Then in 2020 I told my wife I was going to see a different dermatologist than those three and try to find out exactly what it was. I went to the Clinic and told them I wanted to schedule an appointment to be seen, but not with any of the three whose names I gave the nurse doing the scheduling. She said okay and told me there was a new dermatologist who had just begun working at the clinic a few months before. She said his name was Dr. Allan Reck and I told her that would be fine, since I knew he was not one of the three.

When I went into my appointment, I met a fairly young, very personable, man that I instantly took a liking to. He asked if I had ever had a complete dermatology check up and I told him no. He said, "Well, you are going to get one today. Take off your clothes and put on this hospital gown." When I said "OKAY," he left the room and I changed into the gown.

He came back in and took a small, high powered, magnifying

glass and started at my scalp and began a very careful and meticulous examination. As he went all around, and down, my body, he was asking me about my family history concerning cancer.

He finished the exam with a careful look at my toes and the soles of my feet, and then said, "Ron, your skin is in excellent condition, especially for your age. (I was 78 years old then.) He said that my skin was completely clear except for the spot on my forehead.

I asked him about that, and he said, "Ron, that is definitely skin cancer. I'm really glad you came in when you did. It is in the early stages, but it is cancer; and if it was left alone, you would develop some serious skin cancer of your face."

I asked him what we were going to do about it, and he said he was going to give me a prescription for some very strong medicine called "Flurouracil" cream in a tube. He said I was to treat the area once a day for three weeks, then stop all treatment for four weeks. At the end of four weeks without treatment I was to come back in and see him. I was not to use it for more than three weeks because it was a very strong medicine.

He then proceeded to explain to me how the medicine would work. It would not affect or damage any healthy tissue even if it was right next to the cancer tissue. It would, however, affect the cancer tissue, and that area would turn a bright red as if it had been scalded or something. There would be no pain, and I was to cover the area around the cancer tissue well in order to make sure I got all of the "margins" clear. Once I finished the three weeks of treatment the redness would diminish in a couple weeks, and soon it would disappear completely.

VICTORY OVER THE BATTLES

I left the dermatologist's office and went to the pharmacy and got my "Fluorouracil." On the way out to my vehicle I started to have a "pity party." That is where you are feeling sorry for yourself, and it is the smallest party in the world, with only you and the Devil in attendance.

I was complaining to the Lord about my status at the time. I said, "Lord, why do I have cancer again? I just had it in my eye a year ago, and now I have it again on my forehead. It's a different type, but it is still cancer.

The Lord spoke to me, (No, I didn't hear "voices," but a very definite impression on my heart and mind.) and He said, "What are you worrying about? It's JUST cancer." That literally stopped me dead in my tracks, and I replied, "You are right, Lord, and I am sorry. You have delivered me from many things, and that includes cancer. If the Devil wants to attack again, he will be defeated again." Since that time, I have had no doubts on the outcome.

The following Sunday I informed our Church about what it was, what we would be doing, and what would be happening. The Church was very gracious and understanding about it all, and very faithful in keeping me in prayer all the while that my forehead looked like a boiled lobster. I never missed a class to teach, nor a sermon to preach, and the people were faithfully in support of me during the entire time.

After the three weeks of treatment, I quit applying the medicine. About a week later the red was diminishing and by the time I went back to see Dr. Reck my forehead was completely clear. He examined it very carefully and said, "well, Ron, the cancer is completely gone." My question is, of course, "Well, why should it not be? After all…. Cancer is JUST cancer… and God is STILL God!" (By the way, that's where the title for this book came from, when God said that to me on my way to my vehicle from Dr. Reck's office.)

The Devil is a very persistent enemy, however. He doesn't stop.

However, God is even more persistent, and He does not stop either. He is always there to bless us, and to help us, if we will call upon Him in faith.

The following year of 2021 I was checking my face and forehead. I saw the same kind of rash on the right side of my forehead as I had the year before on the left side. I was very suspicious of what it was, but my thinking was far different than it was the last time.

I looked closely at it and thought, "Well, Lord, if the Devil wants another defeat, I'm willing to go through this again as long as you go with me." I wasn't trying to be flippant about it, and I certainly wasn't trying to minimize or make light of the seriousness or danger of having cancer again.

I called the dermatologist's office and told him what I had found. He asked me if I had any of the "flurouracil" left from the previous time and I told him yes. He reminded me of the treatment (every day for three weeks, then nothing for the next four weeks, followed by a visit to see him.) I acknowledged that and began the treatment the next day. He also reminded me that the medicine would not affect the good tissue but would turn the cancerous tissue a bright red.

I alerted the Church and asked them to keep me in prayer again. Sure enough, a few days later the right side of my forehead looked as if I had scalded it. It was bright red again like the left side had been the year before. I went through the required time of treatment, and after the four weeks of waiting, and the doctor's visit, he told me the cancer was all gone again and I was cancer free again.

We thanked the Lord and praised Him for His Faithfulness. For me, personally, one of the things that was most impressive to me was the peace and calm I experienced during the entire ordeal. As I said, I certainly was not trying to be flippant about it, but I was completely confident of what God could, and would, do if it was in His will, and if I would have faith in Him.

I did have faith in Him, and my faith never failed me. Nor did the object of my faith, which is my God. My faith never failed me, and God turned my trials into triumph. Instead of an object of fear and despair, He turned my fight against cancer into an object of victory and praise that is a great testimony to share with others. Perhaps, as you are reading this, you may need that testimony to encourage you in a battle of your own. If so, please try to remember that …..cancer is JUST cancer… And God is STILL God!

The war is not over because we win some of the battles, however. We must be persistent in our care of ourselves, and our willingness to have regular appointments with qualified medical personnel. That way a person is "on top of things," so to speak, if they do encounter something truly serious.

I know there are some Christians who refuse to go to doctors because they believe, for some reason, it is an "evidence that their faith is weak." I totally disagree with them on this because of what the Word of God says, and the fact that we can stand on the promises of that Word. We have to look at the entirety of the Word, however, and not just the portions that people think instruct them to "declare the Word of faith" over their problem. God cannot contradict God by speaking "conflicting truths" in His Word.

One of the specific pieces of evidence of this fact I found in James 1:17, which says, "Every good gift and every perfect gift is from above, and *cometh down from the Father of lights,* (God) with whom is no variableness, neither shadow of turning." Now it says, *"every good gift and every perfect gift,"* and that certainly includes the gift of medical knowledge about such things as cancer treatment, heart problems, diabetes, and other such things is a "good gift," then we must realize that this knowledge comes from God.

Looking for more scriptural verification of the origin of medical knowledge and experience brings us to James 3:17. That says, *"For the wisdom that is from above* is first pure, then peaceable, gentle, and easy to be entreated, full of mercy and good fruits, without partiality, and without hypocrisy."

Now here are just a few things that certainly fit into that category. One is taking a lump out of someone's breast that saves them from terminal breast cancer. Two is doing coronary stints on someone's heart that saves them a coronary heart attack and adds years to their lives. Three is properly described medication that controls a person's blood sugar level and the diabetes that accompanies it when it is out of control.

I certainly am not advocating medical sciences to in any way take the place of faith in God. Far from it. Rather, I am advocating you have a relationship with God, through Jesus Christ as your Lord and Savior, then praying and utilizing the wonderful things (like medical knowledge and expertise) to complement your faith.

I was by-vocational for forty-four years before I retired from the hospital, I worked in. I was a surgical technician and spent those years helping in literally thousands of surgeries that helped many people have longer and better lives who were suffering from the diseases we spoke of, as well as dozens of others. During that time, I also saw multiple cases of people who waited too long to get treatment and died of something that could have been healed completely, or at least had years added to their lives if they had gotten medical treatment sooner.

So, I am sincerely encouraging everyone who reads this to avail themselves of all the medical help they can get for their medical needs, while they can get it. I am also encouraging you to make sure you have a true born-again relationship with the Lord Jesus Christ. No matter how much medical help you get, we are all going to die eventually.

In Hebrews 9:27, God says, *"And as it is appointed unto men* (mankind) *once to die, but after this the judgement."* There are two inescapable appointments you and I, as well as every other person who comes into this world, are going to keep (and not be late for) and those are death and judgement. My word of encouragement to you is to be sure you are prepared for both appointments now since you will *never know when* you will be called to keep them.

Another thing we all need to be prepared for is to fight the same battles all over again as long as we must do so. I speak from experience in this, also.

In 2022 I was once again checking my face concerning the cancer when I noticed just a little rash. I went to the dermatologist again, and again he diagnosed the skin cancer was back. It was on the bridge of my nose and on my cheeks under both eyes. It was pretty severe on the cheeks, but the medicine worked well, and after the prescribed treatment it was once again pronounced healed. Of course, the first thought that came to me was, "Oh no, not a third time." I knew that was simply the Devil trying to discourage me.

Realizing this, I had a word of prayer thanking God that it had been caught again so it could be treated. Then the thought came, "What if it keeps coming back?" The answer came from the Lord, "Then we just keep fighting the battle until we win the war." I was, and still am, satisfied and content with that answer. I don't have the assurance that I will never get cancer again, but I do have the great assurance that God is the answer to it if I do. He is the answer to every need a Christian has and will be faithful every time we trust Him. In Malachi 3:6, He says, "For I am the Lord, I change not." In Hebrews 13:8 the Bible says, "Jesus Christ the same yesterday, and today, and forever." What a sure and unfailing promise we have when we trust Him.

THE FINAL ANSWER

Last summer (2023) we received word that Arlee's last living sister, Jackie, who lived in Idaho, had advanced cancer. I called her and visited with her. She was 86 years old, and she said the doctor told her she had advanced cancer with only about six months left to live. I asked her when the Doctor had told her that and she said, "About four months ago."

I asked if I could speak to her about something personal and she said yes. I told her if the doctor said she only had about six months left, and he told her that about four months ago, then she would have only about two months or so left. After she acknowledged that, I spoke to her about her (and every person's) greatest need in life, and that was to know Christ as Savior before death.

I briefly explained about the glories of Heaven and the agonies of Hell. I then asked her if she would like to pray right them and escape Hell's agonies and be assured of Heaven's glories. She said she definitely would, and so we prayed. It was amazing to see a dying 86+ year old woman instantly become a child of God, a spiritual babe who would never suffer eternal death.

I had known Jackie since I started dating Arlee when I was twenty and Arlee was seventeen years old. Jackie was twenty-six, and at the time of our conversation this past summer, she was eighty-six. She was never interested in anything spiritual, including during any of the conversations I tried to have with her during the fifty-five years Arlee and I have been Christians. I was so thankful to the Lord when Jackie responded to our conversation this past summer. When we finished praying, I asked her if she sincerely meant what she said in her prayer. She said she was definitely sincere about what she had prayed, and she thanked me for sharing it with her.

After the conversation and prayer Arlee and I discussed the situation and decided we would drive out and visit her before she passed. We drove out and spent two days with her, which I sure am glad we did.

She and Arlee had been very close growing up, and I wanted to help both of them as much as I could.

While we were there, Jackie was very weak and couldn't walk more than a few steps, and she was on constant high oxygen all the time. She and Arlee spent their time visiting during the day, and later Jackie's two sons, Richard, and Jimmy, came by and visited after they got off work.

After the two days we left on the third morning and came home. We had a great trip home and visited about the goodness of God and the pleasant visit we had with Jackie and her sons. We had very little sadness about Jackie's status because we knew she had no future in this life in her current status, and that she had a home waiting in Heaven where there is no sickness, or weakness, or death. We could praise God and encourage each other because we knew what Jackie's immediate future held, and we were rejoicing because she did not have long to wait.

About six weeks after we got home, we received a call from Jackie's sons. They said Jackie had just passed away and they thanked us for coming and visiting her before she did so. We reassured them that the pleasure and privilege were all ours. Of course, it was more of a blessing to us than to them because we knew the eternal value of that visit and the phone conversation preceding it. Arlee and I simply give all the glory to the Lord for another soul rescued from Hell and given a home in Heaven.

We have one more soul to look forward to seeing when we get to Heaven. As I have told Arlee many times, God is just adding more individuals to our "welcome home party" when it comes to our time.

So, what difference does it make, or what does it matter whether it is heart attack, car wreck, or cancer? None of them are trivial matters to be taken lightly, nor to be flippant about, as I've said before. They, and hundreds or thousands of others as serious as they, are life and death matters that are to be taken very seriously.

Beyond all that, however, is the inescapable fact of inevitable death. "As it is appointed unto man once to die and after this the judgement." Jesus asked the question in Matthew 16:26, "For what is a man profited, if he shall gain the whole world, and lose his own soul? Or what shall a man give in exchange for his soul?"

One of the greatest mysteries of life is the basic fact of the spiritual realm. That is the fact that those things that can't be seen, touched, or heard are the most valuable and precious things that we can ever have access to, or experience in life. Things like the human soul, the love of God, eternal life, a home in heaven, sins forgiven, a deliverance from Hell; and dozens or hundreds of others just like them. None of these things can be subject to sight, sound, or touch in the physical realm; but all of them are eternal treasures that are far beyond the value of any "treasure" man may pursue of a wordly nature.

That is what was so great in Jackie's choice to accept Christ as Savior in the last couple of months of her life. It was greater than everything else she ever did in her entire life of eighty-six years. Now, since she made that decision, and left this earthly life, she entered directly into the presence of the Lord in Heaven's glory where she will enjoy all of the blessings of the spiritual realm for eternity.

That's why Jesus asks us the question, "What is a man profited, if he shall gain the whole world, and lose his own soul? Or what shall a man give in exchange for his soul?" Satan deceives billions of people by distracting them from the truth. He does that by blinding them to the gospel (good news) of Jesus Christ. Much of that occurs because of the negligence of Christians who have the truth but don't have the motivation to share that truth.

That's the reason for the theme of this book, "….its JUST cancer…." and God is STILL God." It matters not what people must go through here in this life as long as they truly believe God is greater than any "thing," and will trust His plan and purpose for their life.

I am not even implying that it has no value or importance to them, their family and friends, or perhaps even multiple other people. I am stating that according to the Word of God and the perspective of eternity, the only eternal consequence it will have is how it is used, or not used, for the glory of God, and the benefit of themselves and others they may be able to influence during those times.

A man who had one of the greatest Christian testimonies I have ever known was a man whom I pastored back in the late 'seventies. His name was Les Williams, and he had one of the greatest, and most pleasant dispositions I have ever seen.

He also had a multitude of major problems in life physically. He was an older man, married, and with adult children. His family were all Christians as far as I know. I did not know the kids, but I pastored Les and his wife for about two years. He was crippled on one side and had to use two of those "forearm crutches" that you must put your forearms down through to use.

He had I.B.S. (Irritated Bowel Syndrome) which could, and would, hit him at any time. They drove one of those high-topped vans where they could walk upright in it because sometimes the bowel problem would hit while they were driving, and he would have to pull over to the side of the road and go back and use the "porta-potty" they always carried with them.

I don't recall some of the other things that he suffered from, but he bore them all very all. I never saw Les mad, or negative, or in a bad mood. The only time I ever saw him in tears was when he was weeping over someone he knew was not saved, and Les carried a tremendous emotional and spiritual burden for them.

I never once heard him complain, and anytime he talked about his physical condition it was with a smile, and an acknowledgement of his acceptance of God's will concerning it. Why was that? Because, according to Les, He knew what he had to look forward to in Heaven.

As I said, I was their Pastor for two years, and after they moved out of our area and transferred to a different Church up by where their kids lived in central California, I often wondered if maybe our roles should not have been reversed. I thought maybe Les should have been my Pastor, and me his parishioner because of all I learned through knowing him. Knowing Les, though, he would have been the last one to agree with that.

God taught me many things through my association with Les Williams. One of the most important was that I truly wish multiple more Christians could have the attitude and disposition on life that Les had. That is including myself at the head of the line.

I was praying about this very fact one day, and I said, "Lord, I would really like to have a disposition and attitude in life like Les Williams has." The Lord spoke to my heart and asked me, "Would you be willing to go through what Les has gone through, and endure what Les has had to endure?"

I had to think about that for a while before I answered, then I said as honestly as I knew how, "Lord, I don't know if I would be willing to do that, or not. I think I will be happy with what you have given me, and with my own status in life."

That ended that train of thought and I have never had any regrets about the discussion and conclusion that I came to. I know God accepted it because it was sincere and spoken in full faith. I also know I do have the blessed assurance Les had in life, without all the problems and trials he had to deal with. I consider myself as being very blessed by God because of my relationship with God.

In conclusion, let me come back to you who are reading this. Are you facing some "mountain" of difficulty in your life? Whether it be sickness, or disease, or relationship problems, or financial difficulties; or whatever it may be. Please remember this: the world has all the problems, but God has the ANSWER! His name is Jesus! Have you trusted Jesus as your Savior, and do you know you have a home in Heaven's glory? Do you have the blessed assurance that He is in control of everything, and that *He will not fail because he cannot fail!*

I used cancer as the main illustration of what many people face in life, and how debilitating it can be to them. I, and my family, have had much exposer to, and many experiences with, cancer so I believe it gives me a knowledgeable "platform" to speak from. I would just like to re-emphasize the fact that ....cancer is JUST cancer....and God is Still God!!

www.ingramcontent.com/pod-product-compliance
Lightning Source LLC
Chambersburg PA
CBHW051643120626
46551CB00015B/2197